Furniture Manufacturing
in the
New Millennium

First Edition

Thermwood Corporation
Old Buffaloville Rd.
Dale, Indiana 47523

© 1998 Thermwood Corporation

Printed in the United States of America
First Edition Printed 1998

ISBN 0-9665693-0-X

Forward

Ken Susnjara, President of Thermwood Corporation, with his book *Furniture Manufacturing in the New Millennium*, has provided a valuable service to furniture manufacturers seeking to survive in today's competitive world. This book is of value to manufacturers considering a purchase of a CNC machine as well as for those manufacturers currently using these machines in their production. A book authored by the president of a major CNC manufacturer is immediately suspect. One expects it to be heavily slanted to the author's machines, simply a sales brochure in book format, point out the features of the manufacturer's machines and deficiencies in all others. Susnjara has generally succeeded in navigating the fine line between advocating one machine and the technology common to the industry.

Without a doubt, not all readers will agree with Susnjara's methods of calculating costs of parts, by which he essentially demonstrates that setup time for a machine results in the major cost component. This conclusion is significantly different that the generally accepted viewpoint that the faster the machine cuts parts, the better the result on the bottom line. The equation presented in the first four chapters challenge this belief and offers sufficient evidence that the furniture industry should at least look at their costs in a different manner by plugging their specific numbers into these equations. It is suspected that if this were done, there are many manufacturers who will need to rethink the basis for many of their equipment purchases.

Furniture production is undergoing a fundamental change with the lower number of parts per cutting. Susnjara shows that with a batch system of producing parts, using a series of one-function machines that require handling of parts and setup time changing from one part to another part, cost per part increases significantly when the number of parts produced is reduced from 1,000 to 100 per batch. It is shown that using a machine having a faster feed speed to cut the parts does little to reduce the cost per part. However, significant reductions in the cost per part are possible, even with small numbers of parts per run, if the setup time for the machine can be reduced. From Susnjara's perspective, this is the advantage realized by CNC routers, not the faster run times. Reducing the time to set up the machine when changing from one part to another significantly reduces the cost per part. This reduces the manufacturing costs for the producer and provides the opportunity for significantly affecting the bottom line.

A furniture fabrication cell is discussed in one of the chapters. This is a revolutionary concept for the use of CNC routers in which all parts of an article of furniture are produced on one machine as opposed to making interchangeable parts, each with a different machine. Susnjara believes it is now time for the furniture industry to move from making interchangeable parts on a variety of task specific machines and assembling the parts into the finished piece on a production line to making furniture in dedicated fabrication cells. These fabrication cells would perform all machining processes on a part on a single machine and changes from one part to another part on the same machine could occur with essentially no setup time. An easy to use software program is provided to allow readers to evaluate this concept in their own situation.

Manufacturing cells have been a research and discussion topic throughout the furniture industry for a number of years but to date have not been widely accepted. The furniture industry has been notorious for the absence of an innovative spirit – "if my competitor is doing the same thing I am doing, there is no reason to change what I am doing." As Susnjara points out in numerous places in his book, this is not the way the industry will survive and thrive in the new competitive arena. If fabrication cells, or manufacturing cells, or whatever the term ultimately adopted, is instituted by a company, and Susnjara's thesis is correct, that company will enjoy a significant competitive advantage which will either force others out of business or force them to adopt similar practices. Whether the furniture industry that the proposed changes in manufacturing concepts is warranted remains to be seen.

Finally, Susnjara includes a chapter entitled "CNC Router Design" that provides an excellent overview of the various technologies included in router design and is required reading for anyone contemplating purchase of a CNC router. This portion of the book could have obviously become a sales pitch for Thermwood routers. With one or two exceptions, Susnjara has avoided this trap in discussing various engineering choices available in commercial routers. Susnjara discusses a variety of engineering methods to accomplish the same end result and the positives and negatives of these choices. As Susnjara points out, the only truly correct way to judge the various technologies used by the CNC manufacturers is to observe the results. This chapter is a must read for the individuals contemplating purchase of a CNC router.

This chapter also provides the pros and cons for a number of different design methods to accomplish the same task. The author state that there are many technical factors that can be addressed in more than one way and he provides the advantages and the disadvantages of the various ways. For example, massive machines are accurate but usually have a limitation in the rate of acceleration and deceleration due to the mass. What is needed is a rigid, lightweight machine that does not sacrifice accuracy in obtaining high rates of acceleration and deceleration. Another section of this chapter is devoted to various types of drive mechanisms employed to move the machine. The pros and cons of each method are discussed, Also covered is the whip in the lead screw and various methods employed by the machine manufacturers to compensate for this whip. Other topics covered are spindle design and spindle bearings, lubrication techniques, part hold down methods, and CNC controllers.

This book will undoubtedly find many critics within the furniture industry. It is not a traditional textbook but it is not blatant sales literature for the author's company. Whether the reader agrees that the proposed changes in furniture manufacturing techniques to encompass a fabrication cell is warranted, the book introduces innovative and revolutionary ideas, which should be obvious to all readers.

M. W. Kelly
NC State University
May 1998

Table of Contents

Introduction

Great difficulty produces great opportunity. If this is true, the furniture industry in the U.S. offers an incredible opportunity, because at least today it is experiencing great difficulty.

Woodworking today uses essentially the same methods as it used fifty years or even a hundred years ago. Of course, the methods have been refined and modernized, but the fundamental structure and operating methods of the wood industry are little changed.

Until about fifteen or twenty years ago, there was little reason to change. The methods worked and a reasonable business could function using these methods. Then things began to change. Fundamental factors began to modify the economy in which the furniture industry operated. First, business became international. No longer could you simply compete with a few local companies who operated pretty much the same way you did. Instead, you were now forced to compete with companies that operated in countries where lumber was almost free and labor was even cheaper. Sure they had to ship their product here, but their starting cost was so low that they could ship it here and still undercut your prices.

At the same time, business in the U.S. was becoming more competitive. Just-in-time production methods and a drive for low inventory levels were just not compatible with the normal production structure in a woodworking plant. Instead of cutting 5,000 or 10,000 suites once or twice a year you were now cutting 500 suites every month or two.

To this, technology added a further burden. New machines were much more technical requiring a higher level of skill and technical knowledge. Computers, networks and advanced communications increased the intensity and pressure of daily business. It was more than most could handle.

The results were not unexpected. 4,000 furniture companies turned into 2,000 in about ten years. The consolidation continues. Surviving companies, with very few exceptions are doing very poorly by modern standards. Return on investment of 1, 2 or 3% just doesn't get anyone excited. Large conglomerates tried to buy up a multitude of furniture companies and use economies of scale to reduce costs. Dismal results soon had them searching for greener pastures. The best and brightest young students moved into more exciting areas with better growth prospects. The furniture industry has all the signs of a dying industry. Will the furniture industry go the way of the television with low cost foreign companies dominating the market?

Perhaps, and perhaps not. I believe it depends on the fundamental decisions made in the next five to ten years. If the industry stubbornly holds on to the past, they are doomed. If, on the other hand they are willing to consider a fundamentally different structure, perhaps they can survive and maybe even prosper.

What is a "fundamentally different structure"?

If you look at efforts to improve productivity in the woodworking industry, you will find companies trying desperately to gain a percent or two. After all, for some companies this could double their profits. To survive they need to be searching for 25, 50 or 75% improvements not a percent or two.

To most people this sounds ridiculous and impossible. If you are striving for one or two percent it *is* impossible. But if you are aiming for those higher numbers they are well within you reach.

The company I work for builds machine tools. Machine tools are not much different than furniture. The machines are made up of a multitude of machined components assembled by hand into a final product. Furniture is made up of a multitude of components hand assembled into a finished product. The difficulty in improving productivity in building machine tools is about the same as the difficulty in improving productivity in building furniture.

Despite this, we were able to reduce the labor per machine by half in less than three years and reduced it by half again on certain machines. That is a 75% reduction. It is not impossible!

Just after the Berlin wall came down, we were introduced to one of the largest defense contractors in Russia. In a desperate quest for business to replace their defense work, they began machining parts for our machines. The savings were astounding. A part that cost us $1,000 to have machined in the U.S. could be purchased for $2 in Russia. The quality was as good or better and the delivery was reliable and yet today we buy nothing from them. In fact, if their product were free we would still not buy from them. We can produce the part ourselves for less than the shipping cost alone.

Think about it. If they were a competitor, they couldn't compete.

I think the furniture industry can not only compete but can become a highly profitable growth business. To do this they will need to address the fundamental structure of their industry. If you are trying to gain a percent or two, you can pretty well do things the same as you have been, just do them a little better. If you are trying to gain 25 or 50%, you must pretty well abandon your current thinking and start from the basics.

We've done this successfully in our business and I did it in one other area, a furniture company of sorts.

In the mid 1970s, stereo consoles were a significant business. I was retained by a major consumer electronics company to design, build and run a stereo console factory for them. They wanted to produce a product that was substantially better quality and substantially lower cost than their competitors. Traditional methods simply wouldn't work.

We designed a product that was somewhat unique because it was folded up using a molded plastic shell. The really unique aspect, however, was the design of the production plant.

In the planning stages, we modeled the plant along traditional lines and then tried to operate it. There was no way to achieve the results we needed. We then abandoned that approach and built a single production line similar to that found in an automobile plant. The line cycled every minute. The case was assembled and the top fitted, it was finished through a seven step finishing process, the electronics were installed and tested and the product was packaged. When it first started out, it produced a completely finished, packaged and 100% tested stereo console every minute. Eventually it was able to produce two consoles every minute.

As we were designing the plant we were assured by many knowledgeable people that it could not work. Every objection you can think of was offered. How do you keep from painting the grill cloth under the console grill? You can't get a finish schedule that will work on this line. You can't fully test the electronics in one minute. The biggest objection we heard, however, was that any problem anywhere on the line would shut down the entire factory.

This was true. If any department had a problem it would shut down everyone. When each department runs independently, problems do not have nearly the serious consequences. This means that it is much more acceptable to have problems in a traditional structure than in the single line structure. In practice, the line almost never shut down. Because the consequences of a problem were so great, each department put incredible effort into totally eliminating any problem that might shut down the line. I doubt seriously if even half that effort would occur in a traditional furniture plant.

For several years the venture was extremely successful, returning a profit each year equal to the total plant and equipment investment. A 100% return on investment. Only after it was turned back to the owners were more traditional methods added. As this occurred, fortunes declined until the facility was sold.

Are we suggesting that furniture be built like automobiles? Not at all. The high volume world of stereo console production does not exist today.

We are simply suggesting that other fundamentally different approaches be considered. In this book, we hope to give you some analytical tools you can use to evaluate different structures and approaches to major improvement. We hope to provide ideas and concepts that are not common in woodworking today. The same approach will not work for all companies. All companies that plan to survive, however, must have a strategy to dramatically improve productivity.

In this book we will focus mostly on the area of machining components. Many of the concepts will work in other areas of the company, however, getting the fully processed parts to the assembly area at the lowest cost is the core of a furniture manufacturing company. We will also introduce you to a new concept in furniture building which is technically possible today and may hold great promise for the future.

We will approach this from a mathematical and logical viewpoint, however, we will also discuss some of the human aspects of these programs. These human aspects have a strong bearing on the success of productivity enhancing efforts. If people's natural human tendencies will cause productivity to improve, it will be much easier to achieve your goals. These natural human tendencies are determined by the corporate structure. If people are naturally trying to make your programs work, the structure is correct. If your people are fighting your efforts it is not their fault, it is yours. The structure and philosophy of most companies cause employees to mistrust management and fight change. It is difficult enough to fight the market, but if you have to fight your own people in addition, your chances of success are slim.

The single biggest obstacle to improvement in the woodworking industry is attitude. There exists within the industry a accepted formulae defining the "correct" way to do things. These methods have been passed down from generation to generation. Also passed down is the belief that if you simply follow the formulae everything will be all right.

Everybody pretty much uses the same thinking and the industry gets a great deal of security from this collective knowledge. Sure, it takes much time and experience to gain the knowledge, but once it has been won, you have the magic formulae to success. Unfortunately, this is no longer the case. Pretty much everyone using the formulae are failing. If not failing, then certainly not prospering like many other industries.

Examining new fundamental structures robs you of the security offered by following the accepted methods. There is security in emulating those that went before you, but it is false security. There really isn't any security in business today and if you feel confident and secure you are vulnerable.

We will attempt to provide you with both insights and new ideas. We will try and illustrate these as carefully as possible. But, if you don't approach these new ideas with an open curious mind, they will do you little good. For the remainder of this book, we ask you to abandon your current thinking and ideas and examine the new concepts carefully. Think about them and imagine them working.

The current thinking, structures and philosophy used by the woodworking industry in the U.S. today will likely not work in the future. It has failed almost half the companies in the industry in the last ten years and it will fail most others. Each company will need to change. Not small changes but fundamental core changes to the way business is conducted. It is time to start seeking these new ideas. We hope this work can provide you with a good starting point.

Chapter 1

The Formula

Chapter 1

The Formula

We are going to begin with a simple basic formula to define the cost of processing a part through a production center. This formula is deceptively simple when you first look at it. Once we begin to examine it more carefully, we will see that it is actually much more involved than it first appears.

The cost to process a part through a production center is:

Processing Cost = Machine Cost + Labor & Overhead + Tooling Cost + Handling Cost

In this formula we focus on the manufacturing cost through a production center and are not considering material costs. To get the actual part cost it is necessary to add the material cost to the processing cost through each production center. When comparing one manufacturing structure to another, it will be necessary to not only compare the sum of processing costs to each other but to also consider the impact of the structure on material costs. In some cases, a manufacturing process may require less material or lower cost material and this factor must be considered to obtain a reasonable comparison.

Let us now analyze each of these costs in more detail.

Machine Cost

Processing parts at slow speed through an expensive machine will cost more than processing it through a low cost machine at high speed. At least this is the general feeling of most of the industry. In truth, however, this may not necessarily be true.

The wood industry relies heavily on getting machines that are as fast as possible and as low cost as possible. These two criteria are the major factors in determining which of the machines being offered is most desirable. This thinking and these factors greatly influence the development effort of machine manufacturers since they are the basis by which machines will be judged and purchased by the market.

For a continuous production of a single part, these factors are, in fact, the major points to be considered. As the production run size decreases, other factors gain in importance and eventually as the batch size gets small, these other factors overshadow the speed and machine cost.

The actual machine cost per part is a combination of factors. A general formula for machine cost per part is:

Machine Cost = Capital Cost + Maintenance Cost + Floor Cost

Capital Cost

Capital cost is the actual cost of owning the machine during the time it is processing the part. But even here, it is not quite that simple. If a machine processes a part in one minute the cost of processing the part may not be the cost of owning the machine for one minute. If the machine is only used to make one part per year, the machine cost for that part is the cost of owning the machine for one year, not the cost for one minute.

There are several factors that must be considered. The first cost is the actual price of the machine. This is the purchase price plus installation. This is generally the amount that the accountants capitalized on the company's books. If a machine costs $90,000 and it cost $10,000 to install it, they will capitalize $100,000. The machine purchase is not an expense. You paid $100,000 in cash but received a machine worth $100,000. Instead of cash, which is an asset, you have a capital asset.

The accountants will now depreciate the machine. This is based on the theory that each year the machine will be worth less than the previous year. The amount of value that the machine loses each year is called depreciation and this is an expense.

There are several ways of depreciating a piece of machinery. First, a useful life is assigned to the machine. This life is strongly influenced by both tax law and Generally Accepted Accounting Practices. If a company is making money, they will generally want the life to be as short as possible. This makes the depreciation as high as possible. This higher cost from depreciation reduces earnings and thus reduces taxes. Obviously, the taxman would like as long a life as possible for the opposite reason. If a company is losing money, they might want a longer life so that depreciation cost is reduced helping reach for break even. In actuality, there is not much freedom in assigning a depreciation life to a machine.

So, from the standpoint of actual machine cost, the depreciation should provide a reasonable annual expense level that we can use in our formula. But again, it is a little more complex than that. If we financed the machine, we also have to pay interest on the amount of money we borrowed. This interest is an expense in addition to the depreciation and must be included. If we did not finance the machine we do not have the interest expense, however, we still have a certain cost for the use of capital. If we did not use our money to buy the machine we could have put it in the bank and earned a return. The common term for this is the "opportunity cost" of money. Since we did use the money, we will not earn that return and so the money we didn't make is actually a cost for the machine. Another way of looking at this is if we didn't buy the machine we would have this money. Since we did buy it we don't have the money so it should be treated as part of the cost of owning the machine.

To calculate the opportunity cost, we take the interest rate times the average amount of money tied up in the machine. Using straight-line depreciation, the average amount of money tied up in the machine is half the original cost of the machine. If we finance the machine, we will be making payments and so the actual interest will be highest at the beginning of the payments but will be reduced as the principal is paid off. The average interest is then the interest rate times half the original cost of the machine. As principal payments are being made, the equipment is being depreciated so, for a machine that is financed, we can assume that there is no opportunity cost of money for the principal.

We could be somewhat more accurate by using the exact depreciation level and interest cost each year, however, the results will then depend on where in the life cycle of the machine the calculations are made. Since we are trying to compare basic manufacturing structures to each other, these additional complexities will only make it more difficult to determine the most cost effective methods.

For our purposes we will assume that the interest cost in either case is the interest rate times half the cost of the equipment.

We are now to the point where we can state:

Capital Cost = Depreciation + Interest (paid or lost)

Maintenance Cost

Maintenance cost is relatively simple to calculate. It is the cost of maintaining the machine over a period of time. To get a true cost, you must take the entire maintenance department cost, labor, overhead, parts, etc. and distribute the appropriate part of this entire cost to each of the machines using some formula. Assuming the formula is fair, you will come up with maintenance cost for a period of time, i.e. a year.

Floor Cost

Floor costs is another concept that most managers don't pay much attention to but it can have a major effect on both costs and attitudes. The formula for floor cost is:

Floor Cost = Cost of Factory Space + Carrying Cost of Inventory

The theory here is that there is a certain cost associated with the space occupied by a production center. To the processing cost we should also add the cost of the space and the carrying cost associated with any material inventory required to support the production center.

The same arguments used for determining the capital cost of the machine can be used to determine the capital cost of the space occupied by the machine and it's supporting inventory. In addition, we must add interest costs of the inventory. Obviously, if the inventory wasn't required by the production center, we wouldn't have to pay to keep it in place and costs would be lower.

As you can see, this is getting quite complex and we aren't even finished with the first factor in the Processing Cost. It is important that all of this be considered. Most of these factors have very little effect when production runs are very long and they have generally been discarded as immaterial. When production lots become smaller as they have done in the woodworking industry, these factors actually become dominant. If you ignore them, you will be totally unable to see major potential for improvement.

At this point, we have examined each of the factors needed to determine Machine Cost. As an example, let's calculate the annual Machine Cost for a sample machine. Although these numbers may vary quite a bit, for our purposes let us use a machine and installation cost of $100,000 and an annual interest rate of 10%.

Straight Line Depreciation $100,000, 10 Years = $10,000 /yr

Interest cost = 10% X $50,000 = $5,000 /yr

Capital Cost = Depreciation + Interest = $15,000 /yr

For purposes of this example let us assume a maintenance cost is 5% of the machine cost:

Maintenance Cost = $5,000 /yr

This number will depend greatly on the machine you selected and the size and efficiency of your maintenance department.

Finally, we will calculate Floor Costs assuming a building cost of $25 per square foot for a building with a 25-year life, straight-line depreciation. Let us assume that at an average $10,000 worth of inventory sits in front of the machine and that the machine and inventory occupy approximately 2,500 square feet.

Space Cost = 2,500 Sq Ft X $25 /Sq Ft cost = $62,500

Depreciation = Space Cost ÷ 25 Year Life = $2,500/Yr

Capital Cost = Average Space Cost X 10% = $31,250
X 10% = $3,125 /Yr

Inventory Carrying Cost = $10,000 X 10% = $1,000 /Yr

In this case, the Floor Cost is:

Floor Cost = Cost of Factory Space + Carrying Cost of
Inventory

Floor Cost = $2,500 + $3,125 + $1,000 = $6,625 /Yr

We can now determine the Machine Cost per Year as follows:

Machine Cost = Capital Cost + Maintenance Cost +
Floor Cost

Machine Cost = $15,000+$5,000+$6,625 = $26,625/Yr

From here we must now try and determine how much of this amount to charge against a particular part. We could simply divide this total by the total number of hours in a year to determine the cost per hour. This, however, doesn't work. For example, if we only produced one part per year, that part would only be charged with a tiny fraction of the real cost of owning the machine. To properly analyze the production structure we must charge the cost of owning the machine to the work it actually produces. Obviously, the more parts the machine produces the lower the cost per part and the fewer parts it produces the higher the cost per part. We have formulas here to determine exactly how much these differences are.

There are a couple of ways of approaching this question. First, we can try and estimate the total number of hours per year that the machine is actually producing parts and divide the annual machine cost by this number to obtain a cost per hour. We can then multiply the processing time for a part by this number to obtain the cost of processing a part through this machine. This approach will yield reasonable results provided that the time required to set up the machine for any part is essentially the same and that the production lot size is also generally the same. If on the other hand, it requires an hour to set up the machine for a two part run, this approach will yield a cost which is much lower than it should be.

A better approach is to determine the total number of hours each year that the machine is either being set-up or running and then dividing the annual machine cost by that total to obtain the machine cost per hour.

In our example, let us assume that the machine is either running or being set-up 75% of the total time. Ignoring holidays and overtime, which tend to cancel each other out, we can say that:

Total Hours per Year = 40 Hr/Wk X 52 Weeks = 2,080 Hr / Yr

If we use the machine 75% of the time:

Machine Hours per Year = 75% X 2,080 = 1,560 Hr/Yr

We can now determine the machine cost per hour as follows:

Machine Cost / Hour = $26,625 ÷ 1,560Hr = $17.07/Hr

We still have to determine the machine cost per part. This requires that we determine the time required to set up and run a lot of parts and then divide this total cost by the number of parts processed to determine the cost per part.

Let us continue our example by calculating the machine cost per part for two different sized production runs, the first with 1,000 parts and the second with 100 parts. We will use a 1 hour set-up time and a 10 second per part processing time. First, let's calculate the cost for a 1,000 part run. The total time required for this run is one hour for set-up plus 10,000 seconds or 2.78 hours for run time. The cost per part is as follows:

Cost of Run = (1 Hr Set-up + 2.78 Hr Run Time) X $17.07 /Hr = $64.52

Machine Cost per part = $64.52 ÷ 1,000 parts = $0.065 per part

Now, let us perform the same calculation for a 100 part run. In this case there is still a 1 hour set-up time but run time is only 1,000 seconds (100 parts times 10 seconds per part). This is .28 hours. The cost per part is then:

Cost of Run = (1 Hr Set-up + .28 Hr Run Time) X $17.07 /Hr = $21.85

Machine Cost per part = $21.85 ÷ 100 parts = $ .22 per part

In these examples, a part run in quantity 100 is THREE TIMES more expensive than a part run in 1,000 quantity. If the machine were ten times faster, which would be seen by the industry as a major advantage, per part cost would still be $.18. In this example the conventional wisdom that a faster machine is always much better absolutely doesn't work. At this point we have only examined the machine cost, one of four cost factors in the overall processing cost of the part. Once we have examined the rest of the cost factors we will perform more of this type of analysis to try and understand how different approaches can affect the processing cost. This example is simply a quick view to show the magnitude of differences that result from changes in volume and to point up that accepted truths in the industry may not hold up to careful analysis.

Labor and Overhead

The next major factor in determining processing cost is labor and factory overhead associated with that labor. The labor cost normally associated with a production process is called "Direct Labor" because it is a direct cost of production. Factory overhead is the general factory expenses that cannot be associated with a specific production run. This includes light, heat, electricity and certain supplies. The most common way of accounting for factory overhead is to take the total factory overhead for a period of time and divide that by the average number of direct labor hours worked during that period. The result is an overhead rate per direct labor hour. Each time a direct labor hour is used to produce a product, the overhead cost associated with that direct labor hour is also charged to that product.

Some factories pay their people based on the number of parts that they produce. They are paid for each piece produced. In this case, it is generally not possible to associate overhead with a direct labor hour. This situation can be handled by dividing the factory overhead by the total production payroll and determining an overhead rate per dollar of direct labor payroll.

The true per hour cost for an employee is actually higher than the per hour rate that the employee is paid. To the direct pay, you must add the cost of fringe benefits such as insurance, holidays, vacation and the like. Add to that the factory overhead rate per hour and this total cost per hour is commonly called the burdened labor rate and includes the direct pay, cost of fringe benefits and overhead rate. This number is generally developed by the accounting department of most companies and will generally be adjusted once or twice a year. For our purposes we can simply use the accepted number in your factory, although there are pricing techniques which rely on unbundling and treating each of the components separately.

To determine the labor and overhead cost for processing a part through a production center we must consider three separate cost areas. These are set-up cost, processing labor cost and material handling and removal labor cost. For this analysis, we will consider the set-up labor and overhead cost and the processing labor and overhead cost in this area and we will address the material handling labor and overhead costs in the section on handling costs.

The formulas for this are straightforward:

Labor and Overhead Cost = Set-up Labor and Overhead + Processing Labor and Overhead

If the same people that set-up the machine also run the machine, it is simply a matter of multiplying the total man hours devoted to setting up and running the production run by the burdened labor rate. In many factories, however, the people that set-up the machine are not the same people that run the machine. In many cases the pay rates are different and so this difference must be considered. For this reason, we have separated the two activities, set-up and processing, into two separate areas.

Some companies consider setup people indirect labor and do not associate factory overhead with their time. Although this is a valid approach from an accounting perspective, it will tend to mask the true costs associated with short production runs. We will assume that setup labor is direct labor in this analysis, however, if you feel it necessary to treat it as indirect labor, a separate indirect labor rate can be used with the software package covered later in this book.

When two different groups are required, another factor may occur. If the machine operator simply watches while the machine is set-up, his or her cost must be added to the cost of setup. If not, then a certain amount of time is lost returning to the machine or moving to another assignment. On short production runs, these factors can become significant. In presenting examples, I will mostly ignore these effects, however, they will increase, perhaps significantly, the cost of shorter production runs. The differences should be dramatic enough without these additional factors that we can make our points without the extra complexity of these additional considerations.

Let us use these formulas to calculate labor and overhead costs for our example. In the example we will use a burdened labor rate of $30 per hour. Many companies will have a rate well under this number and some may have a higher rate. As we develop some of the new production methods, they will use fewer people than current systems. Fewer people mean fewer direct labor hours to absorb existing overhead costs. This translates into higher overhead rates per hour and thus higher burdened labor rates. By using a $30 number, we are using a reasonable average and can ignore this effect. In actual practice, however, as we become more productive and require fewer direct labor hours, those hours will cost more because the overhead will be spread over fewer total hours.

We will use the same rate for both setup and processing although in many cases the setup rates are higher. This will tend to make short production runs look slightly better than they really are, however, they will look so bad anyway that the slight difference will not be a factor.

Let us again look at both a 1,000 part run and a 100 part run. For a 1,000 part run, it requires an hour set-up and 2.78 hours processing time so the cost is:

Labor and Overhead = (1 Hr Set-up + 2.78 Hr Run Time) X $30 /Hr = $113.40

Cost per part = $113.40 ÷ 1,000 parts = $0.11

Now let's look at the same situation with a 100 part run:

Labor and Overhead = (1 Hr Set-up + .28 Hr Run Time) X $30 /Hr = $38.40

Cost per part = $38.40 ÷ 100 parts = $0.38

Again, the cost per part for the short run is over three times higher even though the part was run on the same machine at the same speed.

Tooling Cost

Most processes use some type of tooling. There is a cost associated with specifying, purchasing, mounting, sharpening and replacing these tools. We have included tooling in the base formula because in some circumstances the cost of tooling differs enough between alternate production structures that it must be considered. For our purposes, we will be comparing different factory structures using essentially the same machining processes. In the processes we will examine, there will be little difference in tooling costs from one structure to another. Therefore, we will not take tooling costs into consideration as we examine the various alternatives.

If you are trying to determine the specific cost of a part, you will need to carefully examine the tooling costs. In many processes the tooling cost is a significant part of the overall processing costs and must be examined carefully. Also, if you are going to use these formulas to evaluate a process or production structure where tooling cost, life or other factors are not essentially the same, you will need to include a tooling analysis as part of your evaluation. When you do these analyses, examine not only the cost of the tools but also the labor and machine time required for the tooling change, assuming this change occurs during a production run. If tool changes occur only during set-up, the tool change time should be included in the overall set-up time.

Handling Cost

This is an important concept based on the traditional layout of a wood furniture plant. There is a cost associated with moving the parts from one production center to the next. For purposes of this analysis, we will add to each production center the costs associated with bringing the material to the production machine from wherever they were located before. The cost of removing the finished parts will be associated with the next production center.

To determine the cost associated with handling the product we will use the formula:

Handling Cost = Equipment Cost + Labor and Overhead

For purposes of these calculations the equipment costs include the depreciation and capital costs as described earlier, however, now these are applied to the material handling equipment. This can be a fork truck, conveyor or other machines.

It is important to take this cost into consideration since a structure that does not require material handling, for example a production cell does not incur these costs between production centers.

The best way to determine the handling cost per part is to determine the total handling cost required to move an entire production batch and then divide this number by the number of parts that were moved. Here again, batch size will have a major impact on cost. For example, if you normally move parts using a pallet and fork truck, and let us assume that you can stack 500 parts on a pallet, then the cost to move one part or five hundred parts is the same. That is the cost to move one pallet. On a per part basis, however, the cost per part is five hundred times more if you are only moving one part.

Let us plug some numbers into the formulas to continue with our example. Let us assume that the fork truck or material handling equipment has a cost of $20,000. In this case we will use machine cost and capital cost but we will not assign specific floor space to the material handling effort.

Machine Cost = Capital Cost + Maintenance

Capital Cost = $2,000 depreciation + $1,000 opportunity cost + $1,000 maintenance = $4,000/Yr

Capital Cost per Hour = $4,000 / 1,560 = $2.56/Hr

We will again use the $30 burdened labor rate to calculate labor and overhead costs. The total cost per hour for equipment, labor and overhead is $2.56 plus $30 or $32.56. Let us assume that it takes 10 minutes (.17 Hr) to move a pallet and we can put 500 parts per pallet, maximum.

The calculations for handling 1,000 parts are:

Handling Cost = 2 trips X (.17 Hr X $32.56) = $11.07

Handling Cost per Part = $11.07 ÷ 1,000 = $.011

Now let's do the same calculation for 100 parts. This time it only takes one trip.

Handling Cost = 1 trip X (.17 Hr X $32.56) = $5.54

Handling Cost per Part = $5.54 ÷ 100 = $.055

The impact here is even greater. It costs five times more per part to move the 100 part lot as it does to move the 1,000 part lot.

Let us take a look at the total processing cost. Here is our basic formula:

Processing Cost = Machine Cost + Labor & Overhead + Tooling Cost + Handling Cost

We will ignore the tooling cost so plugging in the numbers we have developed yields the following processing costs:

1,000 Part Run

Processing Cost/Part = $ .065 + $ .11 +$ .011 = $.186

100 Part Run

Processing Cost/Part = $ .22 + $ .38 + $ .055 = $ .655

Eighteen cents versus sixty-five cents for the same part run at the same speed through the same machine. The difference here is structure. In this simple example using reasonable numbers, the cost of one structure is over three times more expensive than the other. At 1,000 parts or more, the initial structure actually makes some sense. If your volume has dropped, however, the old structure no longer works. If you are going to produce parts in 100 quantity you will need to find a structure that will at least restore the costs associated with your old structure. If you are just starting out and these are the levels you can operate at, you still need to compete with companies that operate at higher levels. No one can operate a business where costs are three times higher and survive very long.

To understand this cost relationship a little better we have plotted the cost per part versus the lot size using the numbers from our example. Here is the result of that plot:

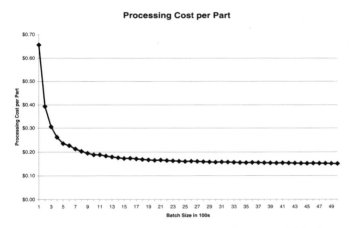

Processing Cost per Part

You will notice that as the volume drops to 100 the processing cost per part skyrockets. As the lot size drops below 100, costs rise even further until a single part run costs almost $68 to process. As you can see, the cost seems to settle out about 20¢ after the lot size increases above 2,500. You will also notice that once the lot size drops below about 500 parts, cost per part rises substantially faster.

Changing the costs of the various parameters will affect the way this chart looks. The chart presented above is simply designed to illustrate the impact of lot size on cost in this particular example. Each set of parameters will have a lot size where the cost per part rises substantially.

This analysis does not take into account another factor which has little effect at large lot sizes but can have a very large cost effect at very low lot sizes. This effect is the tendency to scrap a part or two during set-up on most woodworking machines. Scrapping a couple test parts during set-up will have a minimal cost effect on a thousand-part run. On a hundred-part run, this amounts to two percent of the batch. If the part must run through four or five production centers, this two-percent becomes eight to ten percent which is becoming significant. On even smaller batch size this can become an extremely large cost. The cost is also higher if more than a couple of parts are scrapped at each set-up.

Another cost effect is associated with the practice of running a few extra parts with each batch just in case a few extra parts get scrapped in the set-up or assembly process. Obviously it is more cost effective to run a few extra parts than to set-up each of the machines to make up for a possible shortfall. Again, an extra ten or fifteen parts has little cost effect on a large production run. These extra parts however are ten to fifteen percent of a hundred-part run and are an even higher percent of a smaller batch. These extra parts are either scrapped at the end of the run or must be labeled and stored for the next time the part runs. Either approach adds cost.

This initial chapter should have convinced you that the advent of smaller batches has significantly increased costs. In fact, smaller batches make the more traditional factory structure almost unworkable. The obvious solution is to increase the batch size so that we do not suffer the higher costs. Unfortunately, this is not possible today for many furniture companies. Style changes more rapidly and the cost of finished inventory which cannot be sold is simply too high. Lower inventory requirements means that suits are cut more often and in smaller batches and foreign competition means that most companies offer more styles. More styles that change often also mean smaller batch sizes.

If larger batches are not an answer, then perhaps a modified factory structure can be developed to better handle the small batch sizes. There are a number of experiments going on as the industry tries to develop a reasonable answer to the current dilemma. In the next several chapters we will look at some of these approaches to see if they can help with the problem.

Chapter 2

The Production Cell

Chapter 2

The Production Cell

In this chapter we will examine the detail economics of the production cell approach to manufacturing. Again, we will view both large and small batch sizes and we will run the numbers for a typical example.

The idea behind a production cell is to group all the machines required to process a part together in a single location rather than grouping like machines in departments and routing parts from one department to another. The apparent advantage of this approach is that the handling costs and inventory carrying costs between production centers are eliminated. Since the machines are located in close proximity to one another, in some cases, labor can be shared between machines. This should result in a lower labor cost per part.

The production cell is normally made up of the same production machines that would be used in the department structure so processing speed and set-up requirements will be essentially the same.

The formulas developed in the first chapter also apply to the production cell, however, in this case we will need to analyze the processing cost through several machines to understand the benefits of one arrangement over another.

For our analysis let us consider a part which must be processed through three separate production centers. There are many factors that affect the economics of this process. We will select some typical numbers, however, you must use the actual numbers from your operation to determine the effect of this structure on your costs. Variations in things such as the machine utilization can completely change the results.

We will be using some assumed numbers in our calculations primarily to point out some factors which affect the production cell structure but which are not obvious.

For our initial analysis let us assume we have three machines, one costing $25,000, one costing $50,000, one costing $100,000. Let us use a maintenance cost of 5% of the machine cost each year. Let us also assume that in the department structure each machine is utilized 75% of the time. Let us use a set-up time of 20 minutes for the 1st machine, 45 minutes for the 2nd and 1 hour for the 3rd. Processing time will be 20 seconds for the 1st machine, 15 seconds for the 2nd and 10 seconds for the 3rd. We can also assume that the 1st machine needs 2,500 square feet of factory space, the 2nd needs 2,000 and the third needs 1,500. This space is for both the machine and the staged inventory for that machine. We will again use a $25 per square foot factory cost and $10,000 worth of inventory in front of each machine. We will now calculate the processing cost for a part using the individual department structure. We will begin by calculating the per hour machine cost for each of the machines.

Machine 1, Cost $25,000, 20 min Set-Up, 20 Sec processing time

Machine Cost = Capital Cost + Maintenance Cost + Floor Cost

Capital Cost = Depreciation + Interest = $2,500 + $1,250 = $3,750

Maintenance Cost = 5% X $25,000 = $1,250 /Yr

Floor Cost = Cost of Factory Space + Carrying Cost of Inventory

Floor Cost = $2,500 + $3,125 + $1,000 = $6,625 /Yr

Machine 1 Cost=$3,750+$1,250+$6,625 = $11,625 /Yr

Machine 1 Cost / Hr = $11,625 /Yr ÷ 1,560 Hr / Yr = $7.45 /Hr

Machine 2, Cost $50,000, 45 min Set-Up, 15 Sec processing time

Machine Cost = Capital Cost + Maintenance Cost + Floor Cost

Capital Cost = Depreciation + Interest = $5,000 + $2,500 = $7,500

Maintenance Cost = 5% X $50,000 = $2,500 /Yr

Floor Cost = Cost of Factory Space + Carrying Cost of Inventory

Floor Cost = $2,000 + $2,500 + $1,000 = $5,500 /Yr

Machine 2 Cost=$7,500+$2,500+$5,500 = $15,500 /Yr

Machine 2 Cost / Hr = $15,500 /Yr ÷ 1,560 Hr / Yr = $9.90 /Hr

Machine 3, Cost $100,000, 1 Hr Set-Up, 10 Sec processing time

Machine Cost = Capital Cost + Maintenance Cost + Floor Cost

Capital Cost = Depreciation + Interest = $10,000 + $5,000 = $15,000

Maintenance Cost = 5% X $100,000 = $5,000 /Yr

Floor Cost = Cost of Factory Space + Carrying Cost of Inventory

Floor Cost = $1,500 + $1,875 + $1,000 = $4,375 /Yr

Machine 3 Cost = $15,000 + $5,000 + $4,375 = $24,375 /Yr

Machine 3 Cost / Hr = $24,375 /Yr ÷ 1,560 Hr / Yr = $15.63 /Hr

Handling Cost

For handling costs, let us make the same assumptions we made in the first chapter. Each trip takes 10 minutes (.17 Hr) and we can put 500 parts on a pallet. We will use $30 per hour labor and overhead and $2.56 in equipment and carrying costs for a total of $32.56 per hour. The cost per trip is then:

Handling Cost per Trip = .17 Hr X $32.56 = $5.54

Now, let us calculate the processing cost per part in a 1,000 part lot. Again, we will ignore the tooling costs since we are more interested in comparing methods than in determining an exact per part cost.

Processing Cost Machine 1

Processing Cost = Machine Cost + Labor & Overhead + Handling

Run Time = .33 Hr Set Up + 5.55 Hr run time = 5.88 Hr

Cost of run = 5.88 Hr X ($7.45 Machine cost + $30 Labor / Overhead) + 2 Handling Trips X $5.54 per trip

Cost or Run = $231.29

Cost per Part = $231.29 ÷ 1,000 = $ .23 /Part

Processing Cost Machine 2

Processing Cost = Machine Cost + Labor & Overhead + Handling

Run Time = .75 Hr Set Up + 4.17 Hr run time = 4.92 Hr

Cost of run = 4.92 Hr X ($9.90 Machine cost + $30 Labor/Overhead) + 2 Handling Trips X $5.54 per trip

Cost or Run = $207.39

Cost per Part = $207.39 ÷ 1,000 = $ .21 /Part

Processing Cost Machine 3

Processing Cost = Machine Cost + Labor & Overhead + Handling

Run Time = 1 Hr Set Up + 2.78 Hr run time = 3.78 Hr

Cost of run = 3.78 Hr X ($15.63 Machine cost + $30 Labor/Overhead) + 2 Handling Trips X $5.54 per trip

Cost or Run = $183.56

Cost per Part = $183.56 ÷ 1,000 = $ .18 /Part

Total Processing Cost = $.23+$.21+$.18 = $.62 /Part

This is the processing cost for each part when processed in 1,000 part quantities through a traditional departmental structure.

I will not spell out the detail calculations, however, if the same calculations were performed for a 100 part run through the same three production centers the result is:

Processing Cost Machine 1 = $.38

Processing Cost Machine 2 = $.52

Processing Cost Machine 3 = $.64

Total processing cost = $1.54

Again we see the effect of shorter production runs. The processing cost per part went from 62¢ a part in 1,000 part quantity to $1.54 a part in 100 part quantity. This is over 2 ½ times more per part when processed in the smaller batch size.

Now, let us perform these same calculations for a three-machine production cell. To keep things on a consistent basis, we will assume that all three machines will be set up simultaneously. That is, there will be a separate set-up person on each machine. The set-up time for the entire cell, however, is equal to the longest set-up time for any machine within the cell. This is because the cell cannot operate until all machines within the cell have been set up. The set-up cost is equal to the labor cost for the normal set-up time on each machine plus the machine time for the longest set-up in the cell.

For example, using the numbers in our example, machine 1 requires 20 minutes to set-up and machine 3 requires one hour. The set-up cost for machine 1 is equal to 20 minutes set-up labor and one hour machine time since machine 1 cannot be used until machine 3 is also set-up. In a production cell arrangement all machines must be set-up before the cell can be used.

In this case, the entire cell functions like a single production center so floor space requirements are reduced and only a single inventory of parts is required. This reduces inventory carrying costs. Also, only a single handing cost is required rather than a handling between each machine. Again, this reduces cost.

Processing time for a part through the cell, however, is equal to the longest processing time of any machine in the cell. In this example, even though machine 3 can process a part in 10 seconds, it must wait for parts from machine 1 and machine 2. Since machine 1 can only process a part every 20 seconds, it can only feed parts to machine 2 and machine 3 at a rate of one part every 20 seconds. Effectively, the processing rate for a production cell is equal to the slowest processing rate for any machine within the cell.

To calculate the true processing cost, we need to go back and recalculate the machine costs to take into account the reduced inventory requirements and reduced floor space requirements of the production cell. For this example let us assume that we can house the production cell and the incoming inventory in 3,500 square feet. We will assign Floor Cost to only machine 1 since it needs only apply once for the entire cell.

Production Cell Machine 1, Cost $25,000

Machine Cost = Capital Cost + Maintenance Cost + Floor Cost

Capital Cost = Depreciation + Interest = $2,500 + $1,250 = $3,750

Maintenance Cost = 5% X $25,000 = $1,250 /Yr

Floor Cost = Cost of Factory Space + Carrying Cost of Inventory

Floor Cost = $3,500 + $4,375 + $1,000 = $8,875 /Yr

Machine 1 Cost=$3,750+$1,250+$8,875 = $13,875 /Yr

Machine 1 Cost / Hr = $13,875 /Yr ÷ 1,560 Hr / Yr = $8.89 /Hr

Production Cell Machine 2, Cost $50,000

Machine Cost = Capital Cost + Maintenance Cost + Floor Cost

Capital Cost = Depreciation + Interest = $5,000+$2,500 = $7,500

Maintenance Cost = 5% X $50,000 = $2,500 /Yr

Machine 2 Cost = $7,500 + $2,500 = $10,000 /Yr

Machine 2 Cost / Hr = $10,000 /Yr ÷ 1,560 Hr / Yr = $6.41 /Hr

Production Cell Machine 3, Cost $100,000

Machine Cost = Capital Cost + Maintenance Cost + Floor Cost

Capital Cost = Depreciation + Interest = $10,000 + $5,000 = $15,000

Maintenance Cost = 5% X $100,000 = $5,000 /Yr

Machine 3 Cost = $15,000 + $5,000 = $20,000 /Yr

Machine 3 Cost / Hr = $20,000 /Yr ÷ 1,560 Hr / Yr = $12.82 /Hr

Total Production Cell Costs

Production Cell Cost = $13,875+$10,000+$20,000 = $43,875/Yr

Production Cell Cost Per Hour = $8.89+$6.41+$12.82 = $28.12/Hr

There are several things worth noting at this point. The annual cost of the three independent machines and the supporting inventory and floor space was $51,500 from our earlier example. The equivalent production cell cost is $43,875 for an annual savings of $7,625. This has resulted in a per hour machine cost savings of $4.89.

Now that we have these numbers, we can calculate the processing cost through the production cell. Again we will calculate both a 1,000 part run and a 100 part run. Note that the handling of the set-up costs is modified in this example. Let us start with the 1,000 part run:

Processing Cost = Machine Cost + Labor & Overhead + Handling

Run Time = 1 Hr Set-up + 5.56 Hr Cut Time = 6.56 Hr

Machine Cost = 6.56 Hr X $28.12 Cell Cost/Hr = $184.47

Labor & Overhead = Set-up Machine 1 + Set-up Machine 2 + Set-up Machine 3 + Cut Time

Labor & Overhead = (.33 Hr + .75 Hr + 1 Hr) X $30 + 3 People X 5.56 Hr X $30

Labor & Overhead = $562.80

Processing Cost = $184.47+$562.80+$5.54 X 2 Trips = $758.35

Cost per Part = $.76

This compares to $.62 processing the same parts through the same machines in a more traditional arrangement. This result will surprise many supporters of the production cell concept. Although there are very real savings in inventory costs and material handling, the loss of efficiency dictated by set-up and processing speed more than offsets any savings available.

If the cell were made up of machines whose set-up time requirements and processing rate were near the same, the savings from inventory carrying cost, floor space and material handling could be realized. Unfortunately, it is not normally possible to achieve this compatibility. Also, if a single operator could feed and operate more than one machine in the cell without slowing the overall process, additional savings might be possible.

Let us continue our example by performing the same calculations for a 100 part run. We have already calculated the per hour cost of the production cell as $28.12. The processing cost for a 100 part run is then:

Processing Cost = Machine Cost + Labor & Overhead + Handling

Run Time = 1 Hr Set-up + .56 Hr Cut Time = 1.56 Hr

Machine Cost = 1.56 Hr X $28.12 Cell Cost/Hr = $43.84

Labor & Overhead = Set-up Machine 1 + Set-up Machine 2 + Set-up Machine 3 + Cut Time

Labor & Overhead = (.33 Hr + .75 Hr + 1 Hr) X $30 + 3 People X .56 Hr X $30

Labor & Overhead = $112.80

Processing Cost = $43.84 + $112.80 + $5.54 = $162.22

Cost per Part = $1.62

Again, the production cell yielded a higher processing cost than the more traditional departmental factory structure.

The results of this exercise will change when you put your own numbers in the formulas, however, this example does illustrate that the production cell concept can easily result in higher and not lower processing costs. Even under ideal circumstances, the production cell does not appear to offer a significant potential improvement in processing cost. Under the best circumstances, a slightly better cost structure could result, however, we are looking for a significant improvement in cost. It does not appear that the significant improvement that we are seeking will come from a production cell factory structure.

If you examine all of the examples to this point, you will see that the major problem with smaller production runs and even the production cell is associated with the time required for machine set-up versus the time required for the actual part processing. In the next chapter we will look at the potential for machines with either quick or automatic set-up.

Chapter 3

Machine Set-Up

Chapter 3

Machine Set-Up

In this chapter we will examine the effect on processing cost of a reduced set-up time. The one area that seems to negatively impact processing cost is the time required for machine set-up. This is especially true as the production run size decreases.

It is reasonable to expect that if machine set-up could be reduced or eliminated altogether, costs would quickly drop toward the costs currently experienced in long run production.

How would we expect to reduce the time required for machine set-up?

There are several answers to this question. First, several machine suppliers are offering automated set-up for their equipment. These systems are currently expensive, however, it appears that even at a substantially higher price, these automatic set-up machines may result in lower overall costs. In addition, a new breed of computer controlled routers or machining centers are being offered which offer little or no set-up between part runs.

In this chapter we will examine the impact on processing cost of a quick or automatic set-up machine. We will examine a single production center rather than multiple machines as in the last chapter.

We will use the formulas from the first chapter. We will continue our example, however, we will now assume that instead of $100,000 machine the machine now costs $150,000 for a machine with an automatic set-up feature. We will also assume that this feature will reduce set-up time by 90%. We will assume all other factors such as handling, floor costs and processing speeds are all unchanged. Although these numbers do meet the reasonableness test in today's market, you will need to substitute specific numbers for your application to determine the actual effect on your operation.

Let us begin our example by determining the machine cost. The formula for machine cost is:

Machine Cost = Capital Cost + Maintenance Cost + Floor Cost

Capital Cost = Depreciation + Interest (paid or lost)

For depreciation we will continue to use 10-year straight line. On a $150,000 machine this results in a depreciation cost of $15,000 per year. Interest is the interest you are required to either pay or the interest you could have made on the money used to buy the machine. Over the life of the machine, the average balance of capital associated with the machine is half the purchase price. This is $75,000, which at an average interest rate of 10% results in an interest cost of $7,500 per year. The resulting capital cost is:

Capital Cost = $15,000 + $7,500 = $22,500 /Yr

For maintenance cost we will again use 5% of the machine purchase price or $7,500 in this case. For floor cost we will return to the floor cost calculation from the first chapter. This results in a floor cost of $6,625 per year. The Machine cost is thus:

Machine Cost = $22,500+$7,500+$6,625 = $36,625/Yr

To calculate the machine cost per hour, divide the total annual cost by 1,560 hours based on a 75% utilization. The result is:

Machine Cost = $36,625/Yr÷1,560 Hr/Yr = $23.48 / Hr

This rate, $23.48 compares to a machine cost per hour of $17.07 in the example in Chapter 1. The difference per hour is the additional cost associated with the automatic set-up feature.

Now that we have the machine cost calculated, we can determine the per-part processing cost. We will assume that instead of a one-hour set-up, the automatic set-up feature allows a .1 hour or six-minute set-up. We will use the same 10 second processing time and the same $30 burdened labor rate. Again, we will ignore tooling cost since we are only interested in a comparison. We will perform the calculation for a 1,000 part run first:

Processing Cost = Machine Cost + Labor & Overhead + Tooling Cost + Handling Cost

Processing Time = .1 Hr Set-up + 2.78 Hr Cut Time = 2.88 Hr

Processing Cost = 2.88 Hr X ($23.48 Machine Cost + $30 Labor & Overhead) + 2 Trips X $5.54

Processing Cost = $165.10

Processing Cost = $165.10 ÷ 1,000 parts = $.17 /part

On a thousand part order with a machine which costs 50% more, the per part processing cost is actually less. In Chapter 1 we calculated a processing cost of $.19 per part in 1,000 quantity and here we realized a $.17 per part cost. The only difference between the two examples is the set-up time.

Let us now perform the same calculation for a 100 part run.

Processing Time = .1 Hr Set-up + .28 Hr Cut Time = .38 Hr

Processing Cost = .38 Hr X ($23.48 Machine Cost + $30 Labor & Overhead) + $5.54

Processing Cost = $25.86

Processing Cost = $25.86 ÷ 100 parts = $.26 / part

Although as a percentage this is significantly higher than the $.17 cost of parts in the 1,000 part run, it is significantly below the $.65 per part cost of the standard machine. This is a 60% reduction in part processing cost without changing run quantity. This is the real, significant savings number we are looking for. Using our rigid formula, the per part cost appears to be less anywhere up to 1,000 parts per run.

It appears that reducing set-up time in the short run environment is the critical factor in significantly reducing processing cost.

Furniture manufacturers typically focus on both machine cost and processing speed as the key elements in determining the best machine for their applications. In this example we have shown that set-up time is a more important consideration even though this is typically ignored in evaluating woodworking machines. We used a machine price that is 50% higher with only one advantage, faster set-up. This machine produced parts at a substantially lower processing cost than the standard machine even though the standard machine was significantly less expensive.

To take advantage of this discovery, it is necessary to focus on set-up time as a critical factor when evaluating machines. In addition to the cost, however, the fast set-up offers several additional advantages. A much higher level of flexibility exists with the fast set-up machine. It is no longer necessary to run as many "safety parts" as with the traditional machine. If the run turns up a few parts short, it is substantially less expensive to set-up and run the few additional parts. This can result in significant savings on an annual basis.

Also, it is common that automatic set-up machines result in exact set-up positioning of the heads eliminating the need for one or two scrapped "test parts" after the machine is set-up and adjusted. This again results in significant savings.

Because each set-up is exactly the same, one could expect a generally higher level of part quality and over a period of time, one could also expect lower scrap rates due to improper machining.

We have found a key to substantially lower part costs, however, we are still faced with inventory before each machine and material handling between departments. Wouldn't it be nice to have the advantages of a quick set-up plus eliminate inventory and material handling between departments? Although this sounds like an impossible dream, there is a technology developing which combines the advantages of both. We will examine this approach in the next chapter.

Chapter 4

Combining Operations

Chapter 4

Combining Operations

In this chapter we will examine the idea of producing wood components using a single machine that combines all of the operations needed to complete the part. We will also determine the requirements to operate this machine with little or no set-up.

These seemingly magic machines actually exist and are available from several reputable vendors. They have not been generally considered as a viable alternative to traditional woodworking machines but instead they have been treated as a special machine of their own.

These machines are the CNC router or CNC machining centers as some companies call them. Initially, CNC routers were just that, routers. These machines today, however, are routinely equipped with a wide variety of processing heads and can perform all the operations needed to complete most furniture parts in a single cycle. There is a general understanding that this technology exists, however, there also exists a feeling that substituting a high priced CNC router for more traditional, lower cost woodworking machines is cost prohibitive. CNC routers appear to process parts slower than more traditional machines and there exists a concern that an adequate level of production would be difficult to achieve. Rather than generalize about these points, let us use our formulas to determine the exact results.

In Chapter 2, The Production Cell, we developed an example using three production machines. We will return to that example here, however, we will now consider a single computer controlled machine which can perform all three operations. In addition we will assume that this machine can change from one part to another in five minutes. Both of these assumptions are reasonable with today's technology.

Let us start by calculating the machine cost. For this example, we will use a machine cost of $150,000 although in today's market the actual cost can be somewhat less than this. We will use a one minute processing time which is quite a bit slower than the processing time for the special purpose machines but is typical for three processes on a modern CNC router. We will use 2,500 sq ft of floor space for the machine and inventory and the same inventory level as we used for the production cell. Using our formula that machine cost is:

Machine Cost $150,000, 5 min Set-Up, 1 minute processing time

Machine Cost = Capital Cost + Maintenance Cost + Floor Cost

Capital Cost = Depreciation + Interest = $15,000 + $7,500 = $22,500

Maintenance Cost = 5% X $150,000 = $7,500 /Yr

Floor Cost = Cost of Factory Space + Carrying Cost of Inventory

Floor Cost = $1,500 + $1,875 + $1,000 = $4,375 /Yr

Machine Cost = $22,500+$7,500+$4,375 = $34,375/Yr

To calculate the per hour cost, we will use an 85% machine utilization rather than 75%. A multi-purpose machine is normally used a higher percent of the time than a single purpose machine with the actual utilization approaching 100% in the majority of applications. Let us now determine the total number of hours available at an 85% utilization level.

Total Hours per Year = 40 Hr / Wk X 52 Weeks = 2,080 Hr / Yr

If we use the machine 85% of the time:

Machine Hours per Year = 85%X2,080 = 1,768 Hr/Yr

Now we can calculate the machine cost per hour:

Machine Cost / Hr = $34,375 /Yr ÷ 1,768 Hr / Yr = $19.44 /Hr

For handling costs, let us make the same assumptions we made in the earlier chapters. Each trip takes 10 minutes (.17 Hr) and we can put 500 parts on a pallet. We will use $30 per hour labor and overhead and $2.56 in equipment and carrying costs for a total of $32.56 per hour. The cost per trip is then:

Handling Cost per Trip = .17 Hr X $32.56 = $5.54

Now, let us calculate the processing cost per part in a 1,000 part lot. Again, we will ignore the tooling costs since we are more interested in comparing methods than in determining an exact per part cost.

1,000 part run

Processing Cost = Machine Cost + Labor & Overhead + Handling

Run Time= .08 Hr Set Up+16.67Hr run time = 16.75 Hr

Cost of run = 16.75 Hr X ($19.44 Machine cost + $30 Labor / Overhead) + 2 Handling Trips X $5.54 per trip

Cost or Run = $839.20

Cost per Part = $839.20 ÷ 1,000 = $ .84 /Part

This calculation shows that at a 1,000 part run using the assumptions we have made, the multi-purpose machine is actually higher cost than either the traditional factory or the production cell. Based on previous calculations, the traditional machines could produce a 1,000 part run for $.62 a part, 26% less, and the production cell could produce a 1,000 part run for $.76 a part, 9% less. Now, let us examine this same machine on a 100 part run.

100 part run

Processing Cost = Machine Cost + Labor & Overhead + Handling

Run Time = .08 Hr Set Up + 1.67 Hr run time = 1.75 Hr

Cost of run = 1.75 Hr X ($19.44 Machine cost + $30 Labor / Overhead) + 1 Handling Trip X $5.54 per trip

Cost or Run = $92.06

Cost per Part = $92.06 ÷ 100 = $ .92 /Part

This cost is not substantially higher than the cost of a 1,000 part run. Because of the short set-up time, the difference in cost caused by different sized production lot sizes is much less than either conventional machines or production cells.

The cost of a 100 part run using the multi-purpose machine is substantially below the cost of the same 100 part run on either the conventional machines or the production cell. The cost of processing through conventional machines was $1.54 per part, or 67% higher and the cost of the production cell was $1.62, or 76% higher. The quick set-up, multi function machine produces substantially lower cost parts when operated in small lot sizes despite the slower cycle time and higher machine cost. This provides an opportunity for substantial cost savings if production levels are relatively low.

To understand these calculations better, the following graph shows the cost per part for varying size production batches comparing traditional machines in a traditional` structure, the production cell and a quick set-up multi function machine.

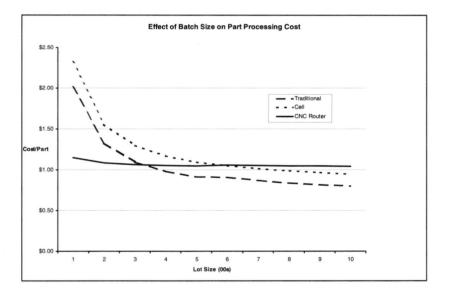

We can make several interesting observations using this chart. First, all three systems are affected by batch size, however, the short set-up requirement of the CNC router causes the effect to occur at a smaller batch size and the cost effect to be much smaller. Using the numbers in our example, it appears that production batches of less than 350 parts are always less expensive on the CNC router. On batch sizes of less than 600 parts, the CNC router is less costly than the production cell but more expensive than traditional machines.

The CNC router has a relatively flat cost curve that does not improve substantially with higher volumes but does not increase appreciably with lower volumes.

For operations that run both large and small production batches, there appears to be a substantial potential for savings using a CNC router in short runs, reaching almost 50% in batches of 100 or less. The potential for loss in long runs appears to peak out at 20-25% in runs of over 1,000 parts.

As we have done in the past, we must again caution you that these examples represent only one set of operating figures. They are what we believe to be representative, however, if your numbers differ from these, the results can be substantially different.

At this point, we can make several generalizations that appear to be accurate.

• Using traditional machines in a departmental structure can result in very high per part costs when parts are produced in small batches.
• Set-up time substantially increases the per-part cost when parts are produced in small batches.
• Set-up time for a production cell is at least equal to the longest set-up time for any machine in the cell.
• Production rate for a production cell is equal to the slowest production rate for any machine within the cell.

We now have a set of formulas with which we can determine part processing costs and we have developed explored one example using these formulas. In the next chapter, we will introduce a software program that is included with this book. It will allow you to input your own numbers and vary those numbers to see how variations affect the processing costs.

Chapter 5

The Formula

Software Package

Chapter 5

The Formula - Software Package

In the world of high volume production, most woodworking managers have a fairly accurate personal intuition about costs. When batch sizes get smaller, however, that intuition either doesn't exist or provides faulty guidance. In this chapter we are going to try and develop some accurate guiding principals about variations in modern woodworking plants. What happens to costs when set-up time changes, or cycle time changes, or machine cost changes or labor cost changes? Is it more important to have faster set-up or faster cycle time?

There is no single answer to these financial questions. Each company will have a different answer depending on the costs and operation of that company. It is important that the furniture manager truly understand what will happen to his or her costs as certain variables change.

To make this easier, we have supplied a simple software program that will operate on a PC running Windows 95. Using this program, your actual numbers can be input into the formulas and you can see the actual costs of processing your product. It is easy to vary each of the parameters and see the effect on the processing cost.

If you sit down with this package and some typical parts for an hour or two, you will develop a real good feeling for how cost vary as different parameters vary within your plant. This should develop an intuitive feeling that is accurate and this intuition should provide you with guidance in your day to day management decisions.

In the remainder of this chapter we will detail the use of the software program.

The program is intended to operate on an IBM PC or compatible running Windows 95. To install the program, place the enclosed floppy disk in the appropriate drive and type:

A:/setup

Where "A" is the drive number. The system will then guide you through the steps necessary to complete the installation.

Once installed and started, the program will display the screen shown here.

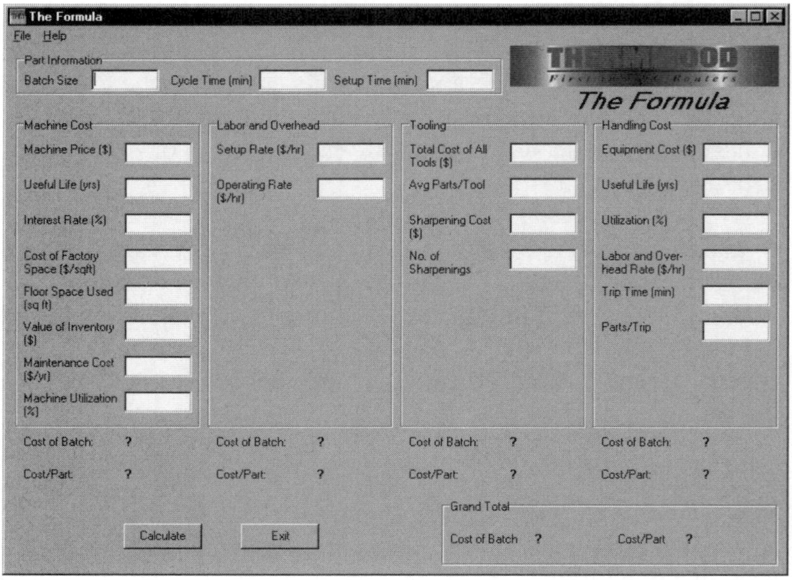

This screen displays the formula as described in Chapter 1. At the top, three fields define the batch to be run. Each of the four cost areas, machine cost, labor and overhead, tooling cost and handling cost have a separate area where all the factors can be input. As the necessary factors affecting the cost area are input, the batch cost and total cost for the area will be displayed at the bottom of the area.

Each cost area has several fields or input boxes. Each field contains a single number that affects the manufacturing cost. You will notice that when you move the mouse pointer over one of these fields, an information box appears detailing the information that should be entered in the box. This is intended to give you a quick review of the appropriate input number. These information boxes are not an adequate substitute for the more detailed information included in Chapter 1 of this book. Make certain that you have read and that you understand the concepts in Chapter 1 before you attempt to use the software package to develop cost data.

At the top of the screen you will find the Part Information area. This area contains three input fields.

Batch Size – This is the total number of parts that will be run using the current set-up.

Cycle Time – This is the time in minutes required to load, process and unload a part.

Setup Time – This is the time in minutes required to set-up the machine for the production run.

Machine Cost

The first cost area is machine cost. There are eight input boxes required to determine the machine portion of the processing cost.

Machine Price – This is the cost of the machine in dollars that has been capitalized and is being depreciated.

Useful Life – This is the period of time in years over which the machine is being depreciated.

Interest Rate – This is the rate of interest that you could have earned on the money used to buy the or the interest you would pay to borrow money to purchase the machine.

Cost of Factory Space – This is the cost to build or purchase the factory floor space per square foot.

Floor Space Used – This is the amount of factory floor space required to house both the machine and the inventory required to support the machine.

Value of Inventory – This is the value of the average inventory associated with the machine in dollars.

Maintenance Cost – This is the average material, labor and overhead cost associated with maintenance of the machine for one year in dollars.

Machine Utilization – This is the percent of the total time based on a single shift, eight hour a day operation (2,080 hours/year) that the machine is either being set-up or is running production. A two-shift operation would be 200%, a three-shift operation up to 300%.

Labor and Overhead

The next area is labor and overhead. In this area you will input the hourly direct labor and the associated factory overhead. Review the description of the labor and overhead rate in Chapter 1 to make certain that you use the full burdened labor rate.

Setup Rate – This is the hourly direct labor cost and the associated factory overhead. If the machine operator must remain idle while the machine is set-up by another, the rate is the total for both the set-up labor and the operator labor.

Operating Rate – This is the per-hour direct labor cost and the associated factory overhead for the machine operator. If more than one operator is required, the number is the total per-hour labor and overhead for all operators required to run production on the machine.

Tooling

The next area is tooling. In this area we will try and determine the tooling cost associated with processing a part. If a part requires more than one tool, we will average the cost and life information to try and develop a reasonable approximation of the tooling cost.

Total Cost of All Tools – This is the total cost to purchase all tools required to process the part.

Avg Parts/Tool – This is the average number of parts that can be processed by a tool.

Sharpening Cost – This is the average cost of sharpening a tool.

No. of Sharpenings – This is the number of times a tool can be sharpened before it must be discarded.

Material Handling

The final area concerns the cost to move material from the previous production center to the current production center. There are six input fields in this area.

Equipment Cost – This is the cost of the fork truck or other material handling equipment required to move material to the production center.

Useful Life – This is the period of time in years over which the material handling equipment is depreciated.

Utilization – This is the percent of a single shift during which the equipment is being operated.

Labor and Overhead Rate – This is the per-hour direct labor cost and the factory overhead associated with the material handling effort.

Trip Time – This is the average time in minutes required to move a skid of material from the previous production center to the current production center and then return.

Parts/trip – This is the maximum number of parts that can be moved in a single material handling trip.

After all input fields have been entered, press the "Calculate" button and the costs will be re-calculated using the current numbers.

Now that you have the basic tool, it is time to play with the numbers. Set up the package with a set of typical numbers for your company. Now, play with the numbers. Change a parameter, batch size for example and see how the cost changes. Change another parameter, machine cost of setup time and again see the part cost change.

Within an hour or two, you should begin to develop a new intuition about how various factors and combinations of factors affect your costs. Playing with the different cost parameters you should be able to develop a real understanding of what different decisions about your operation of your factory will do to your costs.

To develop an even more detailed understanding, perform the calculations for a series of different machines and see how combining operations will affect costs.

This exercise will take some time and effort but the final result will be well worth the effort. The understanding you develop will provide some guiding principals that will make the transition to a more profitable company easy to understand. The intuition will make the difficult decisions clear.

Chapter 6
Achieving Zero Setup

Chapter 6

Achieving Zero Setup

In the earlier chapters we saw the importance of short or zero set-up on part processing costs. In this chapter we will examine the requirements and technology available to achieve fast set-up on a CNC router.

First, exactly what is zero setup? It is exactly what it is called. It is the ability to produce any part required without the need to adjust or set-up the machine. With a true zero-setup machine, production batch runs of one part can be processed at the same cost per part as production runs of a thousand or more.

The real culprit in setting up a machine is the time wasted between completing one part and starting on the next. During this time, the machine is not producing parts but fixed costs and, in most cases labor costs continue. This set-up time reduces the total time available for producing parts and thus reduces the production capacity of the machine.

Although this seems obvious, it is not as simple as it first looks. The problem with machine set-up is not the requirement to perform adjustments or load fixtures; it is the fact that the machine is idle during this process. If the machine could be set-up for the next part while it is processing the current part, there would be no lost time between parts and thus no set-up losses even though some set-up effort is required. Actually, there would be a labor cost associated with this effort but that cost would be limited to the actual direct labor required to perform the set-up function. This is an important idea and we will return to it shortly.

Let us return to basics. There are three requirements for zero-set-up. First, all programs required for any part must either be in the control at the same time or must be directly and quickly accessible by the control without the need to manually load the program. Second, all tooling for any part must be in the machine and directly available to the program without the need to mount or adjust tooling; and third, the machine must be able to hold down all parts without the need to adjust hold-down or locate and set-up fixtures.

If all three requirements are present, you should be able to move from one part design to another without interruption due to set-up requirements. If the machine is also able to perform multiple operations on each part, you have achieved the best of all worlds.

Although this may sound like a dream world, it is actually being achieved on a daily basis in the woodworking industry today. Unfortunately, it can only be achieved in its pure sense for a limited class of parts. There are methods, however, for achieving close to the same result on an even broader selection of part types, however, these require special considerations and somewhat more advanced techniques.

Let's now look at each of the requirements in detail and analyze the available technology for achieving the requirements.

Requirement one, all programs required for any part must either be in the control at the same time or must be directly accessible by the control without the need to manually load the program. To understand the impact of this requirement we must understand the current CNC control system technology.

The original commercial versions of NC or Numerical Controls were developed in the late 1950s and early 1960s. The first company to offer a machine to the woodworking industry based on these controls was Ekstrom Carlson. Their machine was an NC router which used a commercial NC control system.

NC controls did not have any computer functions and could perform no calculations. They used a punched tape that carried the part program as a series of punched holes in a paper tape. This punched tape contained detailed instructions as to the movements of the machine. The control system simply read the instructions and moved as directed by the tape. It is very much like the old fashioned music boxes where pins in a rotating cylinder plucked metal reeds to play a tune. In this case, holes in the punched tape replaced the pins and the NC control replaced the metal reeds.

The original NC controls contained almost no internal logic. This put a great deal of responsibility on the programmer. Acceleration and deceleration for a motion had to be developed by the programmer. For example, if you wanted to program a straight line cut, you needed to program a short line segment at a slow speed then another segment at a slightly higher speed than another at an even higher speed until the speed desired was achieved. Then at the end of the line, you needed to program a series of short line segments at slower and slower speeds until you came to a stop. The sum total of the length of all of the line segments was then the length of the line programmed. If you simply tried to program a line at the speed you wanted, the control tried to instantly move at that speed and either damaged the machine or tripped out the drive amplifier and the machine shut down. As you might imagine, programming this type of control was extremely tedious.

Eventually NC controls were equipped with acceleration and deceleration capabilities about the time a new type of control was introduced to the market. This control was the CNC control. CNC stands for Computer Numerical Control. Unlike the NC control the CNC control was actually equipped with a computer and thus could make certain decisions and perform calculations as the program was executed.

The first CNC control in the woodworking industry was introduced by Thermwood Corporation in 1976. This control was based on the Intel 8080 microprocessor chip and was, in fact, the first microprocessor based CNC control in the world. Thermwood management felt that programming using codes and punched tape was too complex and tedious for most woodworkers and instead introduced a Hand Held Programmer. The Hand Held Programmer was used to generate programs at the machine and was quite easy to use.

The programs generated by the Hand Held Programmer were stored in the control and the operator never actually worked with the numerical code itself. Instead, the operator generated and worked with motions. For example, Move Axis 1, 10 inches in the plus direction at 200 inches per minute. Acceleration and deceleration were handled totally by the control and the operator simply needed to define the moves that were required.

To define the moves, the operator used the Hand Held Programmer to actually move the machine. When the cutting head was moved to the next desired location, the code required to move to that position was programmed by simply pressing an Enter key. The CNC control actually wrote the NC code required for the movement.

Within a few years, commercial versions of the CNC control also became available and other CNC router manufacturers incorporated them into their machines. Manufacturers of these controls opted for a more traditional approach using standard NC code and punched tape.

CNC offered several significant advantages over NC in these early controls. The ability to generate smooth acceleration and deceleration was the most significant, however, the ability to both add to and edit the program at the control were also important. Unlike the early NC controls which could simply execute the program on the tape, some, but not all of the more advanced CNC controls could actually modify the program from the control rather than requiring that a new program be developed and a new tape punched.

All of these early controls were proprietary which means that their programming code and operating systems were written and developed by the control manufacturer themselves. An operating system is a fundamental program that runs things like the keyboard, disk storage and memory handling. In these early days, the most common operating system was CPM and the format used for most operations was based on the Osborne Computer.

Today we take operating systems like DOS or Windows for granted. What we don't appreciate is that, because of these systems, adding hardware, software or features to your computer is quite easy. In the early days, adding features to a control was a difficult and time-consuming task. For example, if you wanted to add a hard disk to the control, you not only had to integrate that hardware but you also had to write not only the software needed for your control to talk to the disk but you also had to write the software needed to operate the hard disk. For this reason, most controls remained rather basic and, in general, controls tended to lag behind the advancing computer technology.

With the introduction of the IBM personal computer and the DOS operating system, an accepted standard was born. Within a few years, some companies, including Thermwood, had converted their controls to this new standard. Unfortunately, most others continued on with their proprietary systems because of the huge investment in both money and time that they had already made.

A major schism now developed. Those companies who adopted the new standard were subject to operating systems written by others, however, they had the advantage of easily and inexpensively adding new features as they became available. Those who continued with their own systems found it technically difficult or impossible to keep up with new advances. For example, early hard disks were 5 megabyte at most. Incorporating these into a proprietary control was a difficult and expensive task. Since the overall volume of CNC controls was small by computer standards, the disk, which could be purchased for a PC at a few hundred dollars might cost $10,000 or more on a CNC control. Within a few years, 10, 20, 50 megabyte disks were available and they quit making 5 megabyte disks. All the work on a 5 megabyte disk was lost and the effort had to start again. Most control manufacturers simply provided enough memory in the control to hold the program and did not offer a hard disk.

Even today, most proprietary controls either do not offer mass storage at the machine or the cost of a hard disk is very high. We are faced with the problem of storing every program we have in the control at one time and most controls don't have mass program storage. Now what?

Actually, the problem is even worse. Early NC programs were very small, generally consisting of a few hundred lines of code. The amount of program storage memory that a control manufacturer puts in the control determines the largest program that the control can run. As long as programs were generated by people, one line at a time, this was not going to be a problem. However, a system called CAD/CAM came along and things became much more complex.

CAD/CAM stands for Computer Aided Design, Computer Aided Manufacturing. These computer programs allowed the part programmer to design a complex part and then create a program to manufacture this part quickly and easily. While CAD/CAM systems make programming easy, they can generate programs that are not necessarily efficient. For example, in generating a curve, most CAD/CAM systems create a series of thousands of very short straight lines all strung together. This creates two new problems. First, the size of a program can become too large to fit into the CNC control memory. Early CNC programs might be one to three thousand bytes long. With most CNC memory being 50 or 100 thousand bytes in size, there was plenty of safety factor. CAD/CAM systems however, routinely created programs of a half a million to a million bytes in size. Even newer programming systems such as automatic trace probes can create programs that are a 100 to 200 million bytes long. It seems that regardless of how big you make the control memory, someone finds a way to create a program that is too big for it.

The second major problem that these huge programs cause is slow execution speeds. Typically, CAD/CAM created programs are made up of a series of very short line segments. Each of these line segments is represented by a block of NC code. In order to execute the program, the control must process hundreds or possibly thousands of blocks of code every inch of movement. This results in several practical problems.

First is simply the speed at which a block of NC code can be processed by the control. If the control is capable of processing a 100 lines of code per second it is said to have a 10 milisecond block processing speed. This is typical today for a reasonably good CNC control. If the program has 100 blocks per inch, the control is limited to 100 blocks of code per second so it can run at one inch per second. This is 60 inches per minute which is rather slow for a CNC router.

The second problem caused by these small line segments is associated with a method that many control manufacturers use to process very large programs. Instead of loading the entire program into the control, they use a separate computer to hold the program and they feed part of the program into the control. While that part is executing, any extra computing time is used to feed additional program code from the program computer to the CNC control. This works reasonably well unless you are running at or near the block processing speed of the control. In that case, there is no extra computing time to download the program. Program execution uses all available resources.

When this occurs, program execution continues until all of the program that has been downloaded is executed, and then the machine stops and waits until more of the program is downloaded. This process is called "filling the buffer" and it is common for most CNC controls that are trying to execute large CAD/CAM created programs.

There is a new type of control that is gaining popularity. These controls are based on the PC and are called PC based controls. They have the advantage of using a common operating system and thus they are compatible with many of the hardware and software packages available for PCs. PCs have become very powerful and this is the reason that these systems work at all. Even with its incredible processing speed, a PC based control is slower than a proprietary control. Although they can handle large programs, they execute them slower than most proprietary controls.

Thermwood, who has always been somewhat of a maverick in this area has approached this problem in a different manner. First, they decided that a single computer could not achieve the required performance so they designed a system that used multiple processors. They created a proprietary system that achieved extremely fast block processing speed, about five times faster than most available systems. This was accomplished by using multi-tasking and breaking the CNC task down into simple components that were each handled by a different task running on the control. This increased operating speed from about 60 inches per minute to 300 inches per minute. Then, they created a system where a very large hard disk (several gigabytes in size) would operate as main memory. This is known as virtual memory and it allows almost any conceivable program to load and operate directly from the control memory. This eliminates downloading buffers and the associated pauses and problems.

To address the compatibly issue, the Thermwood control turned to a standard Pentium computer to handle the operator input and output. This processor shared a buss with the proprietary system so communications between the two is almost instant. The result is a CNC control that can be equipped with most PC hardware at a very low cost but can also outperform most proprietary CNC controls when running large complex programs.

At the time this book is being written, two new features are entering the area of CNC controls, multi-tasking, which we have already mentioned, and open architecture. These technologies are being proposed by several commercial CNC control manufacturers and are available on at least one system already in the market. While the base technology is advanced, the real value of these new capabilities is in the things that they can do for the end user of the control.

Multi-tasking is the ability to execute more than one program at the same time. For use in CNC technology, the multi-tasking must be preemptive. This means that certain tasks have priority and are executed in real time as required and then other tasks are executed as computing resources are available.

One current use of multi-tasking is Thermwood's 91000 SuperControl where multiple programs are executed simultaneously within the control. Control tasks are pipelined. This means that the first program does part of the control task and then passes it to the second program and then to the third and so forth. In this way block processing speed can be increased substantially.

Open architecture means that like a PC, programs not written by the control manufacturer can be run on the control. It also generally means that programmers who are not part of the control manufacturer can modify or add features to the control system without assistance from the control manufacturer. Taken alone, the ability to run other programs would have limited appeal since you would need to stop the machine in order to run another program on the control. When combined with multi-tasking, however, this feature adds a great deal of capability to the system.

The open architecture and PC bus allow a network card and supporting software to be installed on the control. Then, even while the machine is operating, the operator can send or receive messages using E-mail or receive messages or, up or down load part programs from the network server or from another control.

Thermwood currently offers a number of features on its control which rely on both open architecture and multi-tasking. The entire machine operating and maintenance manual is included in the machine control. Even while the machine is processing parts, the operator can access the manual. A search function allows the operator to look for every reference to a word or phrase within the manual and then move to the section of the manual containing the information required. Both text and graphics are included as well as short video clips showing how to perform some of the more complex maintenance procedures and adjustments.

Several background programs operate while the machine is in production. The first is a monitor program that time-stamps every event that occurs to the control and places this information in a file. Each time a part is run, a switch flipped or a control turned the event is recorded. This file can then be accessed through a network and the resulting file used to provide management with detailed, up-to-the-minute information on the operation of the machine.

The second background program tracks tooling. Although it appears to be part of the control, it is actually a separate task. In much of what we are proposing in this book, a large number of tools are used at random to process short runs of a large number of different parts. One of the problems which occurs with this type of operation is tracking tooling life. Normally, the tool will be used until it no longer performs its function properly. The way you determine it is no longer working properly is that the parts it is producing are no longer acceptable. In short run production, scrapping parts is very expensive. This is especially true when machine time has been used to perform several operations and only one operation has been unacceptable.

Most operators do not watch product quality close enough to detect the first time a part is scrap, so you may actually produce quite a few bad parts before the tooling problem is detected. If you are running fifty or a hundred tools in a bulk tool changer, you will constantly be fighting dull tooling. You will also constantly be producing scrap parts.

The solution to this is a tool management program that runs simultaneously with the machine and keeps track of the actual cutting time on each tool. You can then assign a life to each tool. Tool life is determined by experience. As the tool is used, the control subtracts the actual usage from the available life. When all the life has been used up, the control notifies the operator that the tool life has expired and the tool can be changed before it begins to produce scrap parts.

Tooling cost is a major consideration, however, it is better to change a tool before it actually becomes completely dull rather than risk scrapping parts. When you are performing several operation on a part, the value of the part becomes quite high. It takes very few scrap parts to pay for a new tool. In addition, in this type of production environment, the disruptions caused by scrap can be quite expensive.

Another concurrent program in the Thermwood control tracks actual machine usage and alerts the operator when lubrication or routine maintenance is required. Using graphics, it then guides the operator or maintenance personnel through the lubrication or maintenance procedure.

This program helps remind a company of required maintenance but also saves time and money by reducing maintenance or lubrication that isn't needed. Time based systems which, for example, say to perform a procedure once a week will waste effort if the machine was not used for three days that week. If the machine is used two or three shifts a day, once a week may not be adequate. With the maintenance monitoring program, maintenance is called for when it is needed, not too soon and not too late.

These examples show you some of the incredible advances that are made possible by multi-tasking. Multi-tasking is a goal for most control manufacturers and although the examples shown here are currently available from only one company, it will not be long before almost every control manufacturer offers similar capability.

With this background, let us now examine the available methods of achieving our first goal, having every part program available at every machine. Obviously, the most straightforward method of doing this is to have a large enough hard disk at each machine to hold all of the required programs. If the control does not have a hard disk, but can be connected to a PC, the programs can be loaded in the PC hard disk and then downloaded into the control as needed.

If you are going to use this second method there are several considerations. First, make certain that you will not try and run a CAD/CAM generated program with small line segments using this method. The resulting pauses and slow speed will likely be unacceptable. Also, make certain that the connection between the PC and the control is fast. A common way of transferring data between two computers is using a serial port. This is commonly referred to as a DNC link. Although this type of link can move short programs in a few seconds, it can take a very long time to transfer a long, complex program. I have seen a DNC link take a half an hour to an hour to transfer a very large program and this defeats our goal of eliminating set-up. In general, any program you will ever run should be able to be transferred in a minute or less.

Another way of providing a large number of programs to a variety of machines is using a network. Unlike a DNC link, a network can transfer large programs very quickly. In this arrangement, a central computer stores all the programs and each machine control downloads the program whenever it is needed. This arrangement has several benefits.

First, programs are stored and controlled from a central area. If a modification is required to the program, it needs only be changed in one area. If the program is stored on a number of separate machines, the new version of the program must be loaded in each of the individual controls.

This brings up another really fundamental problem that must be addressed. Programs for CNC controls in the wood industry are written in an ANSI standard called 274-D. This protocol defines movement of each of the axes of the machine. The code tells the machine how far to move each axis. A program written for a particular machine will tell it to move a certain amount required to machine a part. The problem occurs when a machine is equipped with more than one head.

When this occurs, the program must not only tell the machine how to move but it must also tell it how far to shift over to move the second or third head over the workpiece. If you are running only one machine, there really isn't any problem. When you operate two or more machines is where problems occur.

The source of the problem is that it is all but impossible to build two machines exactly the same mechanically. Getting the relationship of the heads in several machines to match exactly is not practical today. This means that a program written for one machine will not work on another machine because the amount that the program must shift for the second or third head is different on each machine. Does this mean that a separate program must be written for each machine that a part is to run on? In many companies, programs are developed on a CAD/CAM system and then run through a post processor for each machine. The post processor is a program that understands the mechanics of each machine and adjusts the part program for the actual mechanical dimensions of a particular machine. Thus, there is a separate post processor program for every machine.

Using this method, a single part design program is developed for a part. This part program is then processed through a separate post processor for each machine it will run on. Although this is commonly done, there is a better way.

On certain controls this problem can be bypassed provided the control allows sub-programs to be called within a program. Sub-programs are programs that can be called by other programs. To allow for machine differences, simply write short sub-programs that provide the necessary shift for the machine to move from one head or one tool to another. These tooling programs stay with the machine and are called by the part program any time it is necessary to move from one head to another. These tooling programs are different for each machine, reflecting the actual mechanical configuration of the machine. The program names, however, are the same so that when a program to change from head one to head two is called, each machine makes whatever moves are necessary to shift from head one to head two.

Thermwood has refined this approach in their control by supplying sub-programs called tooling macros that perform these functions. Instead of simply running a separate program to shift the head, the tooling macro adds the necessary moves to the next programmed axis motion, saving time. Overall, there are some major benefits to using a machine resident program to define all machine specific dimensions.

The most obvious advantage is that one program can run properly on every machine. If you think about it, the machines can be quite different and still execute the program correctly. For example, consider one machine where the second head is mounted to the right of the first head and a second machine where the second head is mounted to the left of the main head. Obviously, these two machines are configured quite differently, however, the tooling macro shifts one head right and the same tooling macro on the other machine shifts the head left. Using tooling macros, both machines produce the same part using exactly the same program.

Another advantage occurs when head configuration changes on a machine. For example, suppose a head is replaced on a machine. It is nearly impossible to locate the replacement head in exactly the same mechanical position as the original head. Without exact position, all programs that rely on the head position will need to be adjusted to reflect the new position. If you are using a CAD/CAM system and a post processor, the post processor for that machine must be modified and then every program must be reposted. Some companies have thousands of programs and this can take a lot of time.

If, however, you use a tooling macro to define the head position, it is only necessary to change the tooling macro to reflect the new head position. All other programs that call the tooling macro will automatically use the new position since the tooling macro uses the new position.

This technique is called indirection. It is used commonly in modern computer programming to make changes easier to control. Although it appears to be more work at the beginning, it saves tremendous effort in the long run.

Allowing all machines to use a common program can provide a high level of flexibility and will save many problems associated with running the wrong program on the wrong machine.

There are a few other considerations in this area. One rather obvious consideration is how difficult is it to locate and load the proper program. Many CNC controls can only store part programs with numerical names. This makes the task of locating the correct program more difficult since it is quite easy for people to transpose numbers. Most PC based controls can store programs with alphanumeric names that make them much easier to identify. If the programs can be stored in a directory system as PCs do, structuring is easier. All part programs for each finished product or suite can be stored in a particular directory. Then it is simply necessary to move to the directory for the product you are producing and select the program for the part you wish to make.

The easiest way to select the proper program is using a system such as a bar code reader. Again, you must make certain that the CNC control you are using is compatible with a bar code reader hardware and software. If it is, however, the bar code needed to load the proper program can be printed on the top of the work order for the part. All the machine operator needs to do is scan the bar code and press the start button. The chances of error are almost zero. Also, the process only takes a few seconds rather than several minutes to locate the correct program in a directory structure.

So, the first requirement for zero set-up isn't quite as straight forward as it first appears. Some CNC controls are becoming quite advanced and I recommend that you get the highest level of capability you can with the purchase of a new machine. Also, I would give preference to a machine supply company that offers the ability to upgrade their controls on an ongoing basis. Many of the control capabilities today could not even be imagined just a few years ago. We certainly can't predict what type of capabilities will be available in just a few years. If you can add these new capabilities to a machine you purchase today, you assure yourself that you will not be left with a non-competitive production system in the future. At least for today, however, make certain that your CNC controls can handle large programs, run small line segments from a CAD/CAM system very fast and store and retrieve thousands of part programs very quickly.

The second requirement for zero-set-up is to have all tools required for every part in the machine at one time. The obvious reason for this is to eliminate the time required to change tools between part runs. The idea of having every tool in the machine at all times is the ideal and there are several things you can do to reach for this goal. If it is just not possible, then the next best thing is to provide for very quick tool change between part runs.

Once you have to change tools manually between part batches, however, you add a whole new layer of complexity to the process. First, you must determine which tools must be changed. This takes time and can easily result in mistakes. Then you must locate the proper tooling and you must locate that tooling in the machine accurately. This is much more complex than simply scanning a bar code, loading a part blank and pressing the start button.

CNC routers today can perform a variety of functions in addition to routing. For simple routing, however, high capacity tool changers can easily eliminate the need to ever have to change router bits in the machine. Simple tool changers typically hold five to eight tools. Bulk tool changers can hold up to fifty tools and with a dual installation a single machine can automatically select from 100 different router tools. Few companies require this many different tools.

For use in a tool change spindle, the router bit is secured in a tapered tool holder. The tool holder then fits into a tapered shaft of the spindle and is secured by a set of grippers located inside the spindle. A set of strong internal springs normally hold the grippers up and the tool holder in place. To change tools, the spindle is stopped and a hydraulic or pneumatic cylinder pushes down on the gripper, compressing the springs and releasing the tool holder.

Most companies can get by with just a few router tools. A five-position tool changer can be equipped with four standard common bits and have one position open for custom or shaped tools. Thus most routing can be accomplished with the standard tools and when a special shape is required, the tool and holder is simply snapped into the custom tool location.

Tool selection for line boring is another area that requires some thought. Typically, drill banks are available for CNC routers. These drill banks generally have spindles on 32mm centers so that they can bore multiple holes on 32mm or 64mm centers. This provides for fast cycle time since several holes are bored simultaneously, however, unless holes are always the same size, it does require that tooling be changed each time a new part is set-up.

Tooling set-up in this situation can be somewhat complex and time consuming. Not only do you need to know what size drill bits are required but you also need to know what configuration of drill sizes was assumed by the part programmer when the part program was written. You must know what size drill bit is supposed to be in each drill spindle. This process can be quite time consuming and pretty well destroys our goal of zero set-up.

An alternative is to assume that all holes will be bored one at a time. You can then equip the drill bank with every drill bit diameter from 1/16 inch to 7/16 inch in 1/16 inch increments. On a typical nine-spindle drill bank, you can also add a counter sink and a counter bore. For holes of ½ inch or more, you can use a half-inch router bit, programming tiny circles for larger holes. Be careful when doing this because some CNC control do not produce accurate small circles. Higher quality controls perform the circular interpolation calculations very accurately and will produce very accurate circles even with diameters of 1/16th inch or less. Lower capability controls, however, may produce ragged or egg shaped small circles that will not give you the desired result. If you intend to use this technique, check this out before you purchase a machine.

Using this alternative approach, you will bore holes one at a time. This is slower than boring multiple holes but, overall it can be faster. The reason that boring holes one at a time can be faster than boring them several at a time is that, for a short production run, the time required to determine the correct tooling and then load that tooling will be longer than the extra time required to bore the holes one at a time. A hole can be bored rather quickly. On most parts, unless there are hundreds of holes, the time savings which results from boring several holes at a time amounts to only a few seconds per part. On a hundred or two hundred part run, the total time savings might only be a couple of minutes. This is much less than the time it will require to tool up the drill bank for the part. As a general rule of thumb, on short production runs plan to bore holes one at a time with a standard drill bit layout.

There are several approaches to tooling a CNC router. The most obvious approach is a standard router spindle equipped with a tool changer. A useful addition to this is one or more "piggy-back" routers. A "piggy-back" router is a router spindle, generally smaller than the main spindle. It is mounted to the main spindle using some type of slide so that it can be programmed to position below the main spindle and can be used for routing or it can be positioned above the main spindle so that the main spindle can be used for routing.

The advantage of "piggy-back" routers is that they can be lowered and ready for use in a second or two versus a tool change that requires 15 to 30 seconds depending on the machine.

A drill bank including horizontal drills can also be very useful.

An alternative to this type of conventional tooling is a rotary turret. Rotary turret tooling is currently available from at least two manufacturers and has one major advantage over conventional tooling.

Conventional tooling basically supports the routing process with boring added as an extra. The turret can be equipped with tooling heads that are fundamentally different than routing, sanding for example.

Tool change on a turret occurs by rotating the turret until the desired tool is in the lower working position. Most turrets have eight tooling positions and so can support eight different operations. There is generally a provision for removing a head and replacing it with a different head, however, this can be time consuming on some machines. Thermwood has developed a simple power buss system where the head automatically attaches to the necessary power only in the down, working position. This allows the head to be removed and replaced with another in the horizontal position without the need to make electrical connections. A switch and cam system identifies the head to the control so that the program does not try and run with the wrong head installed. Even with this improved system, changing a head is not something you want to do between part runs.

The turret offers a tooling option that allows us to reach one of our goals, performing all operations in a single set-up. Because of the configuration of the turret, however, there is not enough room for a conventional tool change spindle. This means that tooling must be manually loaded into the turret.

Actually, removing a router bit and replacing it with another is not a particularly time consuming task. Adjusting the new bit so that the length is exactly right can be time consuming, however. This is especially true if you are using a shaped tool or if the tool is going to be used for pocketing. In these cases, the tolerance at which you set the tool becomes the tolerance at which the part is manufactured.

Thermwood offers a system that simplifies this process but it only works for metal bits. They locate a tool length measurement button just off the back edge of the worktable. A new tool is mounted at approximately the correct position but no effort is made to accurately position the bit. Changing a tool this way can be accomplished rather quickly. Before the tool is used a measurement macro, or program, is run. This program moves the tool over the measurement button and lowers the tool $1/10^{th}$ of an inch at a time until the tool touches the button. The control can tell that the tool has made contact because the button is electrically grounded by the tool. This requirement for grounding is why the system is limited to metal, electrically conductive tools.

At this point, the head reverses direction and moves in $1/100^{th}$ of an inch increments until the electrical ground is broken. It then moves back down in $1/1000^{th}$ of an inch increments until the electrical contact is again made. Using the position of the head at this point, it is possible to very accurately determine the length of the tool. This length is automatically loaded into the control's tool length table and all programs that use the tool will be adjusted to reflect the new tool length.

This system can determine tool length within one or two thousanths of an inch. If any type of mechanical switch was used, it would require actual movement to trip the switch. Variations in the mechanical movement required to trip the switch would result in inconsistent measurement of the tool length. This system trades the limitation that it only works for metal tools for the fact that it can measure tool length very accurately.

The goal is to try and equip a machine with all tools required to manufacture all parts. As you have probably determined by now, this is not likely for many larger factories. In a larger factory, however, every machine doesn't have to produce every part. It is possible to create "families of parts" where the basic processes that the part must go through and the tooling required can be automatically available on a machine. It is also possible to modify construction methods and make slight adjustments in assembly design so that the parts can be produced on a standard tooled machine without the need for special tooling.

If the designers and product engineers are aware of the importance of designing the product so that it can be processed on a machine equipped with a standard set of tooling, it becomes much easier to reach our goal. I have seen instances where every part required to assemble an entire piece of furniture was produced on a single machine with a standard set of tooling. If you combine a flexible CNC router with extensive tooling and intelligent product design, you can get very close to reaching the zero-set-up goal if not actually achieving it.

The final requirement for zero-set-up is the ability to hold all parts down without the need to change fixtures or adjust hold-down pods. Can this be done?

Just as with the other two requirements the answer is yes and no. There are a couple of different methods of holding down parts for machining that require no adjustment but each has some limitations. Before we address those directly, let us examine the various methods of holding parts down on a CNC router.

Before we talk about methods, we should discuss the general importance of part hold-down. Most people assume the sole requirement for hold-down is to hold the part in place so that it can be machined and in general, this is true. However, there are different degrees at which the part is held in place. In other words, a part can be held rigidly in place or loosely in place and the result will be different for different materials.

A plywood part being cut for the interior of an upholstered chair has a different size tolerance and surface quality requirement than a carved drawer front for a high-end chest. The result is that a hold-down method that works great for the plywood part will not be satisfactory for the carved drawer front. When we examine the available hold-down methods we must not only examine the techniques but must also determine the type of parts that can be successfully held using the methods.

The major difference between hold-down systems is basically the difference in how rigidly the part is held in place. The material, the cutting tool and the feed speed determine the cutting forces placed on the part when it is being routed. Basic hold-down simply resists the major side force caused by the advancing tool. Thus the part is held in place and the hold-down is considered adequate. The hold-down system resists the major cutting force but may not resist the hammering forces caused by the edge of the router bit hitting the part thousands of times a minute. If the part reacts to these forces, tool marks or cutting marks will result on the edge of the part. In general, these are very small and tend to be consistent around the part.

An even more serious problem, however, can occur when the cutting forces and frequency match the natural frequency of the part and the part and tool begin to vibrate. These harmonics can cause a very poor quality edge. The result of this is a rough cut which only occurs on certain places on the part. The more rigidly the part is held in place, the less likely is this problem.

With these facts in mind, let us quickly look at the different hold-down methods in use today.

Mechanical clamps are the most basic and generally the most rigid form of hold-down. These are available in several configurations. They can be secured to the table top and put force on top of the part clamping it to the tabletop. They can push forward, securing the part against a fence or guide. Clamps can be mechanical or pneumatic and come in a variety of sizes.

Clamps are the only practical method of holding small parts that will receive heavy cutting forces.

The most common way of holding parts on a CNC router is using conventional vacuum. A vacuum pump, which creates the vacuum, is connected through vacuum hoses and a valve to a vacuum fixture. The vacuum fixture generally uses a rubber seal to seal the fixture against the part to be held. When vacuum is applied, the outside air pushes the part securely against the fixture.

The amount of holding force depends on the amount of area inside the vacuum seal. Most vacuum pumps can generate about 10 to 12 pounds of holding force per square inch. A part that has a 12-inch by 12-inch area inside the vacuum seal has 144 square inches of surface. With 10 pounds of vacuum per square inch, the part will be held in place by 1,440 pounds of force. Conventional vacuum can provide a substantial holding force, especially for larger parts.

There are several problems that can occur with conventional vacuum. The vacuum pump generates a fairly high vacuum, however, it does not produce high flow at these vacuum levels. A small leak in the vacuum system will cause air to flow into the sealed vacuum area at a rate which the pump cannot keep up with. This will reduce the level of vacuum and thus the holding force.

This is one of the reasons for the vacuum seal. Without the seal, too much air will leak into the vacuum and the holding force will quickly disappear. There are other places besides the seal area that can generate leaks.

The material itself can be a problem. Some materials are somewhat porous. Certain hardwoods, particleboard and the like can leak enough air through the part itself to cause problems. Unsealed spoilboard materials can leak air and, of course, mechanical leaks in the vacuum system itself will cause problems. Conventional vacuum will work very well when properly designed, properly sealed with the right material, however, it is not the answer to all applications.

Conventional vacuum will generally hold the part firmly in place. When processing hardwood with conventional vacuum, however, additional effort may be required. If the rubber vacuum seal supports the part sometimes it can move slightly, suspended on the flexible seal. Should this occur, a poor quality machined edge may result. There are several solutions to this problem although the most straightforward is to place adhesive backed sandpaper under the part, inside the seal. When pulled down, the part contacts the sandpaper, which holds it rigidly in place instead of resting on the rubber seal.

The major disadvantage to conventional vacuum in a zero-set-up environment is that a fixture with a vacuum seal must be installed on the machine for each part. This seems somewhat inconsistent with zero-set-up.

In some cases it may be possible to devise a fixture seal design that can hold a number of different parts. In this way, you can change from one part to another without the need to change fixtures. With smaller parts, it is possible to fixture a large number of different parts on the router table where any part on the table can be run at random.

There are several systems on the market that eliminate the need for special fixtures by using smaller standard fixtures that are adjusted for each part. The most common system uses small vacuum pods, typically 3 inch in diameter, to hold the part. This system is used extensively on point to point boring machines. The individual vacuum pods are mounted on moving slides. To set-up for a part, enough pods are moved under the part to support it. These are then mechanically locked in place. Some type of locating pin or stop is used to locate the part blank.

The pod system does eliminate the need for individual fixtures but it also requires some effort to set-up. In many cases, it will take longer to set-up a pod system than to change a spoilboard with individual fixtures. The pod system also provides less overall holding force and less rigidity than a custom fixture although it is sufficient for most panel work. The area where a pod system does offer an advantage is where a part will only be produced once. It can be set-up for the part without the need to build a fixture that will never be used again.

Another version of the pod system is the "flip-pod", a system patented by Carter Corporation.. This is a vacuum pod that is machined flat into the tabletop. Any area where you wish to hold a part, you remove the pod and turn it upside-down and replace it. It then sticks above the table about two inches and offers a vacuum pod about three inches in diameter to hold the part. Turning it upside-down opens a vacuum valve inside the pod allowing vacuum to the seal area. Otherwise it is closed and that area of the table doesn't receive any vacuum.

Flip-pods are quicker to set-up than most other pod systems, however, since the pod can only be located in certain areas, it is not as flexible as far as part placement. It is also necessary to provide locating pins for the part.

When dealing with conventional vacuum there does not seem to be a system that can change from one part to another without some type of set-up. Unfortunately, there are many part applications where conventional vacuum is obviously the best method of holding the part for machining.

Although pure zero-set-up can't be achieved with conventional vacuum, there is a way to get most of the benefits of zero-set-up using most of the conventional vacuum systems I have described here. I will return and explain this in just a little while.

The next hold-down system I will describe is also a vacuum system, but it is the first truly universal system. Like conventional vacuum, it also uses a vacuum pump, but it uses a different type of pump. The vacuum pump used for conventional vacuum produces a high vacuum but a relatively small flow. This pump produces a relatively low level of vacuum but at a very high flow. This means that the level of vacuum that it achieves will remain fairly constant even with serious leaks in the system because the high flow more than compensates for the leaks.

Earlier I mentioned that certain materials, like particleboard, are somewhat porous and can leak air right through them. Although this is a problem in conventional vacuum, we actually use this characteristic in universal vacuum. A shallow cavity is machined into a plenum placed on top of the router table. This is covered with a piece of particleboard exposing the entire under surface to vacuum. When vacuum is turned on, air flows through the particleboard into the plenum and into the pump. Flow is so high that a low-pressure area is created on top of the particleboard tabletop. A flat part that is laid on this table will be held in place by this low-pressure area without the need for fixtures or seals.

The amount of force generated on the part is much less than conventional vacuum. The best systems today generate between 2 and 4 pounds per square inch. The 12-inch by 12-inch part that we determined was held down by 1,440 pounds of conventional vacuum will only be held by 288 to 576 pounds of force using universal vacuum. For most flat panel work, however, this is more than enough holding force.

Thus, we have a system that can hold down different sized parts without the need to change fixtures or set-up vacuum pods. Our problems are solved! Unfortunately, this isn't quite true.

If you are processing flat panels of MDF or other composite materials it is close to true. The panel size must be large enough to generate a sufficient holding force but other than that, zero-set-up is easy. In fact, small cuts into the particleboard top don't seem to affect subsequent hold-down of different sized parts. Randomly holding different sized parts every cycle is routinely being done in the industry today using universal vacuum. In these cases zero-set-up for fixtures is both practical and cost effective.

Plywood, hardwoods and other materials present another problem.

Earlier I mentioned that this system relies on a low-pressure area created by air flowing through the particleboard top. What I didn't mention is that this low-pressure area only exists for a few thousandths of an inch above the particleboard surface. For a part to be held in place it must move into this thin low-pressure area. A smooth panel can easily do this. If a panel is warped, it won't move into this low-pressure area so it won't be held down. Conventional vacuum actually has enough force to pull a warped panel flat for machining in many instances. Universal vacuum does not offer this same capability and is highly intolerant of warped workpieces.

Also, if the panel has a rough surface, the roughness holds the panel away from the low-pressure area and the panel will not be held down. This is what happens with most plywood. The rough surface of plywood and the tendency of plywood to warp make it unsuitable for universal vacuum.

This also generally applies to solid woods. Although I have seen people successfully use universal vacuum to hold down solid wood panels, it is fraught with potential problems and will generally fail more often than it succeeds.

So, with universal vacuum we do have an answer for smooth flat panels.

There is another system that offers almost the same capability for plywood and other sheet material that cannot be held by universal vacuum. Again, there are both capabilities and limitations.

This system uses rubber-coated rollers located in front of and behind the router head. Generally there are four rollers, two in front of the head and two behind it. The head moves side to side between the rollers. The rollers move front to back with the head. As the head moves front to back, the rollers roll on top of the part pinning the sheet to the table top.

There are several advantages to this system. First, it can successfully hold down warped parts as long as the warpage is not so great that the part catches on the shields. It can also hold down more than one sheet of stacked material. There are some limitations to the system however.

The biggest limitation has to do with part size. To work properly, a part must be held by at least two rolls. This means that parts need to be at least 12 inches long. Even then, roller hold down will not hold parts as rigidly as other hold-down methods. There are techniques for machining smaller parts using roller hold-down. One method cuts the parts through, except for some thin tabs that hold the part to the sheet. When removed from the machine, the parts are broken out by hand and the tabs sanded off. Another technique that works well for very small parts is to not quite cut all the way through the sheet. Leave .005 to .010 inch web of material that holds all the parts together. Then, run the sheet through a wide belt sander, removing the web holding the parts together. All the small individual parts are now free.

There are also some programming requirements for proper roller hold-down operation and some layout restrictions. When followed, however, this system offers reliable part hold down that needs no set-up between different parts. Again remember, if a very smooth edge is required you need to test the roller hold-down system to determine if it will hold the parts securely enough to get the edge quality you require.

One other thing to watch on a roller hold-down machine. Early designs clamped the rollers to the table using the table slide rails to resist the holding forces. The rails are generally track ways with linear ball bearings. This additional force on the track ways and ball bearings caused premature wear and failure. Newer designs use a separate set of rolls under the table to resist the clamping forces. This does not place additional load on the track ways and bearings and does not reduce their life.

There are some more exotic hold down methods but these are seldom used in the woodworking industry. To summarize where we are currently at, clamps hold a part securely but require set-up. Conventional vacuum using fixtures hold most parts, except for very small parts but also requires set-up. Conventional vacuum using pods hold most larger parts, not as securely as a fixture but also requires set-up. Universal vacuum holds smooth, flat sheets at least 12-inch by 12-inch and does not require set-up. Roller hold down holds sheets at least 12 inches long, does not require set-up but does not offer as rigid a hold-down as some of the other methods.

Unfortunately, there is no one nice neat answer for all parts. There is however, a technique that I mentioned earlier which will allow you to get most of the benefits of zero-set-up even with clamps and conventional vacuum. This technique, however, requires a dual table machine.

Many CNC routers are equipped with a dual table. The generally accepted reason for the second table is to allow one set of parts to be machined while the operator is loading and unloading the second table. Thus the machine never needs to stop for load and unload.

On the surface this looks like a great idea, but like many great ideas it does not hold up to careful analysis. A dual table machine will generally cost about 50% more than the same machine in a single table version. To just break even on the investment, the dual table machine will need to produce at least 50% more parts than the single table version. Since you are tying up more resources with a dual table machine, you really need to produce more than 50% additional parts to justify a dual table machine.

In addition, it requires more time to set-up two tables for production than it requires setting up a single table. The higher production rate must also overcome the additional loss of production time associated with setting up the second table.

Let us use some examples to understand this better. Let us assume a two-minute cycle time and a twenty-second unload/load time. Thus, on a single table machine you will produce a part every two minutes and twenty seconds. One part each 140 seconds means 25.7 parts per hour.

On a dual table machine you can produce a part every two minutes since the machine does not need to wait for the next part to be loaded. For purposes of this evaluation we will ignore the time required for the head to move from the first table to the second table. A part every two minutes means 30 parts per hour or, 4.3 parts more than the single table machine.

In this case, we have paid 50% more for a machine that produces less than 17% more production. Obviously, this is not a good investment.

What if the unload/load time is half the cycle time? Let us assume a one-minute cycle time and a thirty-second unload/load time.

The single table machine will produce a part every 90 seconds or it will produce 40 parts per hour. The dual table machine will produce one part a minute or 60 parts per hour. At this point, the dual table machine is producing 50% more parts than the single table. This, however, only breaks you even. There is no advantage to either machine at these rates.

In general, a dual table machine and machine paced operation makes sense with short cycle times and long unload/load times. It does not normally pay to use a dual table machine for complex parts that have a long cycle time.

Since we are advocating CNC routers that perform several operations each cycle, longer cycle times will be more common, making dual table operation uneconomical in most applications.

There is a place, however, where dual table machines seem to make economic sense. Most dual table machines allow you to operate the machine as a single table machine using either table. You can set up one table and run production while the second table is being set up for the next part. In this way, there will be no delay from the end of the first production run to the beginning of the second one. The savings from eliminating set-up is normally much greater than the savings from slightly higher production speeds which result from dual table operation.

This technique allows you to achieve zero-set-up in those instances where the fixtures or hold-down on the table can't be made truly universal. You will recall that in earlier chapters we showed that it was cost effective to purchase a machine with quick set-up or automatic set-up even if it cost 50% more than normal whenever production batch sizes were small. This same economic analysis applies to a dual table CNC router where the reason for the second table is to reduce or eliminate set-up between parts.

Zero-set-up or near zero-set-up is both possible and practical today. Each of the three requirements is both technically feasible and commercially available today. Mass program storage is available in some controls, right at the machine and is available with many others through a high-speed network. Turret tooling heads, multiple router heads and bulk tool changers allow all or most tools used in the operation to be available by the program automatically. Universal vacuum and roller hold-down provides zero-set-up part hold down for certain parts, or, dual table machines allow fixture set-up during production when these systems are not adequate.

Zero-set-up can work with proper planning. Zero-set-up will provide most companies with the single largest cost savings available in their factory. It is a generally unrecognized opportunity that every furniture manufacturing company should examine very carefully.

To understand the magnitude of zero-set-up, use the software package from the last chapter. Input the current costs for a production center that normally has a long set-up and small batch size and substitute a zero or near zero set-up time. The cost difference will surprise you.

We have talked about several factors affecting CNC router design and use in this chapter. We will again visit these areas later in this book when we talk about CNC router design in detail.

Chapter 7

Furniture Fabrication Cell

Chapter 7

Furniture Fabrication Cell

In the last few chapters we have determined that in short run production, performing all operations on a part at one time on a single machine is generally cost effective. We have also determined that zero or near zero-set-up offers a major cost advantage. We have shown that both of these goals can be reached using today's commercially available machine technology. In this chapter we are going to take these thoughts one step further.

At this point we hope we have convinced most manufacturers that this new technology and the new evaluation criteria can make sense in their operations. As different as these ideas are, they do not address, or challenge, the fundamental manufacturing structure in a furniture plant.

From the beginning of time until the industrial revolution, furniture was made one piece at a time. A craftsman made each part, assembled the parts and finished the piece of furniture. If the part didn't fit he adjusted it until it did fit. He then went to work and made another piece of furniture.

With the advent of the industrial revolution and the invention of the production line by Henry Ford, the building process was broken down into its individual motions. The major manufacturing process changed from manufacturing products to manufacturing parts of products. Individual components were fabricated in batches rather than one at a time. These components were then taken to an assembly line where the end product was assembled from the individual components.

This technical advance relied on a totally new concept. When product was built one at a time, each part was fabricated to fit the final product. If it didn't fit, it was adjusted until it did fit. That part, however, would likely not fit any other end product. For the assembly line concept to work, parts had to be interchangeable. Although we are used to this approach, it was a radical idea in its time and was not universally accepted.

Furniture manufacturing adopted this same philosophy. Instead of building each piece, one at a time, and then assembling these into a finished product, the individual pieces were produced in large batches. The pieces were then taken to an assembly area and assembled into finished furniture.

The reason that these practices were eventually adopted was that it was less expensive to produce each individual component in a batch than to make it one at a time. When the transition first occurred, there was a lively debate as to whether the savings from the assembly line could possibly offset the higher cost of manufacturing interchangeable parts. At first, it didn't, but as manufacturing technology improved, the cost of producing accurate interchangeable parts came down. Today, this is obviously the best way to produce a product. Or is it?

Let us look at some of the problems that result from this fundamental manufacturing structure which the furniture industry adapted back in the early nineteen hundreds.

The most fundamental problem was the same one faced by every other industry that made the transition, how to fabricate accurate interchangeable parts. The parts must be fabricated on different machines with different tolerances and adjustment requirements. Unlike most other industries, however, the furniture industry is working in a material that is not dimensionally stable. Wood changes dimension as its moisture content changes. It grows, shrinks and warps.

This means a part that is dimensionally accurate today may not be dimensionally accurate several days from now when it is time to assemble it. Even if you machine it correctly, it might not be correct in a few days when it is important.

To address this problem we dry our wood and carefully try and control the moisture content. We control the humidity in the factory and carefully stack the parts, sometimes with spacers so that should it gain moisture it does so evenly.

When you produced only one of each part and then assembled them, parts were easy to keep track of. When you produce a multitude of different parts, it is necessary to keep track of the identity of the parts as well as the location in the factory. To accomplish this we develop sophisticated and sometimes complex paperwork systems. Computers allow us to operate these systems quicker, easier and with fewer errors. But, we must keep track of the parts, nonetheless.

We must also store and transport the parts. In the early days, the parts were fabricated right where they were used. There was no need to move them around as part of the manufacturing process. Today we move parts all over the plant. We even move them from department to department to machine them because we group different types of machines in different locations.

The interchangeable part/production line manufacturing system relies on the entire production team. If the person that was supposed to make part "B" doesn't make it, production stops. In fact, if any part of the production process falters, production stops. It is vital that everything keeps working properly and this is a major part of production management's job.

All of these things seem normal and natural. We do them every day and they are the accepted way of operating. It is difficult to imagine things working any other way. It is also difficult to imagine these practices, which seem so natural, as being a problem. At one time, however, these functions were not needed. A craftsman built all the parts and assembled the piece of furniture without the need to track parts, move parts or control plant humidity. In fact, the requirement for doing all these things was cited as a major disadvantage to the new production methods. If one craftsman didn't show up for work, his work didn't get done but everyone else kept making furniture with little disruption.

Interchangeable parts and the production line method won out. It won out because, ultimately, it was more efficient and less expensive. I am now going to suggest that, just as in the early nineteen hundreds, technology is again changing the economics of furniture production.

The methods we currently use are no longer working. When we produced furniture in large cuttings, the system worked reasonably well. Today, however, with small batch runs the problems are almost overwhelming. Most shareholders of furniture companies would make more money by putting their money in a bank CD than they make by investing in a company that builds furniture. We are now at the point where the problems associated with the production line concept have become greater than the benefits of using the method.

At this point we are going to suggest that returning to the original method of making furniture might actually make economic sense. We are not suggesting that we go back to the technology of the eighteen hundreds. We are suggesting that we look forward to a totally new manufacturing technology that will operate using the manufacturing philosophy of the eighteen hundreds but using the technology of the twenty-first century.

Let us try and explain this more clearly. As we have seen, it is possible to perform all machining processes on a part on a single machine. In addition, we have seen that it is also possible to change from one part to another with little or no set-up. This means that the cost of producing parts in batches of one is essentially the same as producing them in larger batches.

If you will recall, the ability to produce interchangeable parts in large batches at a lower cost was the overriding advantage to the production system we use today. If that advantage no longer exists, why continue tolerating the shortcomings of the production line structure? Why not make all the parts for a piece of furniture, one at a time, and then assemble them into a finished piece?

The reason we operate the other way is that, up until now, it has been more efficient to make parts in large batches. But, we have seen that technology has changed that. Today, parts can be manufactured one-up on a CNC router for less than they can be manufactured in small batches using more traditional machinery. Therefore, furniture should be built using this new production approach at a lower overall cost than is normal today.

What we are suggesting is as radical as the change from hand made furniture to production line furniture in the early nineteen hundreds. At this point in the book, most experienced furniture makers should have thought of dozens of reasons why this won't work. We assure you of two things. It will work technically and it is substantially more productive and cost effective.

If we are right, just as the change from hand-made furniture to production line furniture was inevitable, the change to cell-made furniture is also inevitable. The cost savings using this method are substantial. We are not talking about a 2 or 3% savings. We are talking about a 20, 30 or 50% savings.

At this point, we are going to ask that you examine this concept with an open mind. Try and forget everything you currently believe about building furniture and simply try and understand and imagine the ramifications of this idea.

Let us start with the first objection. Building furniture using a cell based on a CNC router is slow. The router can be tied up for hours building one piece of somewhat complex furniture.

This question is based on current thinking about CNC routers and the current attitude about machine speed and its value. These machines are currently viewed as one type of specialty machine that is relegated to a specific task, routing. In the new manufacturing system they are the only machine. There is no need for tenoners, boring machines, chop saws, horizontal borers, molders or carving machines. The Furniture Fabrication Cell is made up of a highly versatile CNC "Furniture Building Machine" and a few pieces of manual equipment.

One cell can produce furniture, but yes it might seem slow. An entire plant filled with cells can produce a lot of product. You cannot operate a factory with one Furniture Fabrication Cell anymore than you can operate it with one traditional woodworking machine. Today it requires a substantial investment in plant and equipment before you can produce the first piece of furniture. With the Furniture Fabrication Cell, the first cell can start producing furniture without the massive investment.

In fact, the capital cost per unit of production may be less with the Furniture Fabrication Cell than it is today. That means for a certain level of production, the Furniture Fabrication Cell production method may require fewer dollars of machine investment than a more traditional furniture factory. Although a single cell may seem slow because of the way it is structured, the Furniture Fabrication Cell is actually a faster production method than furniture factories today.

This concept is similar to the operation of a plastic molding plant. In these plants, large molding machines perform essentially all the major production tasks. Operators at the machine watch over the presses, remove finished parts, and at times perform secondary operations. The entire product, however, is generally produced at one time in a cell like arrangement. Production rates are determined by the speed of the molding machines. The total number of machines in operation determines plant capacity.

A Furniture Fabrication Cell has at its center a Furniture Fabrication Machine. What exactly is a Furniture Fabrication Machine?

We are using the name Furniture Fabrication Machine to denote a special kind of CNC router or CNC machining center. This machine has a number of requirements that differ from its normal use today. It is in meeting these special requirements that the machine becomes a Furniture Fabrication Machine. Note that the requirements that we list here are the minimum requirements. If a machine meets all requirements but one, it cannot function as a Furniture Fabrication Machine.

Here are the basic requirements for a Furniture Fabrication Machine:

Mass program storage, the control must be able to store large carving programs as well as a large number of individual programs

Program calls and sub-routines, a master program must be able to call and execute other programs that can in turn call other programs

Program Stop command, you must be able to instruct the machine to stop program execution within a program until the start button is pressed

The ability to branch within a program on operator input, the part program must be able to branch to another program or another part of the current program based on operator input and then return to the original program.

The ability to output audio instructions to the operator, the program must be able to call audio programs or initiate audio instructions to the operator.

Automatic tool change and mass tool storage, every tool needed for a piece of furniture must be available automatically.
Both vertical and horizontal tables, both the surface and the edge of parts must be available for machining.
Measurement sensor input and decision making power within the program, the control must be able to measure parts and take appropriate action or make necessary adjustments.
The ability to carve, includes fast block processing speed and "look ahead" for minimum lag error.

Let us look at these requirements in more detail, one at a time.

Mass Program Storage

If there are thirty-five different parts in a piece of furniture you will need thirty-five different programs. If some of these programs are intricate carvings, they may be very large, perhaps megabytes in size. Audio instructions, which we will discuss in a few minutes, require large audio files. To function properly, the CNC control must be able to store and quickly retrieve a huge amount of data to function in a Furniture Fabrication Cell. At the time this book is being written, the minimum data storage we recommend is a gigabyte. Two or three gigabytes is much better.

Unless data transfer can be made both automatic and very fast, a system where the mass data is stored off the control and loaded as needed will not work very well. If the operator must either wait for data transfer or participate in the data transfer effort, the overall disruption of the production cycle will be substantial enough to adversely affect both the processing cost and production rate.

Program Calls and Sub-routines

When a program that is running can load and execute another program, this is called a program call. The program that is called and executed is called a sub-routine. This is a powerful capability but all CNC controls are not capable of calling a sub-routine. One program calling another is an absolutely essential requirement of a Furniture Fabrication Machine.

The main program must be able to call a program for each of the individual parts that make up the piece of furniture being built. The main program must also be able to call the audio file to play instructions for the operator. Conditional branching, for example to make a replacement part when a part is scrapped, also requires a program call. Suffice it to say that the program call is an essential part of a Furniture Fabrication Machine control.

Program Stop command

This is another command that some CNC controls don't offer. A program stop is simply a command that stops program execution until the start button is again pressed. Although it seems very simple it would be virtually impossible to operate a Furniture Fabrication Cell without the program stop command.

Each time a part is completed, program execution must stop until the operator removes the part and prepares the next part. A programmed command must be available to provide this pause.

Branch On Operator Input

Everything doesn't always go perfect. When an error occurs or a part is scrapped, the operator must be given the ability to intervene in the sequence of program execution to either redo a part or make a replacement part. This can be done in a straightforward manner by using operator inputs that branch to sub-routines that are designed to handle the special situation. Obviously, to do this the machine control must have the fundamental capability to branch or call a sub-routine based on operator input and then return to the original program and continue.

Audio Instructions

Unlike a simple CNC router that manufactures a part over and over again, a Furniture Fabrication Machine needs to make many different parts in sequence using different fixtures on the table and different raw materials. With a simple CNC router the operator loads a common blank and waits for the machine to process the part. With the Furniture Fabrication Cell, the operator is constantly loading different parts, turning parts over and performing other tasks. It is virtually impossible for an operator to know what to do next without some type of detailed instructions.

The production sequence could be written down, however, the operator will then need to stop what he or she is doing, find the current place in the written sequence and then read and understand the next instructions. This effort can be quite disruptive. After awhile, the operator will try and remember the next step in the sequence so the instructions don't need to be referred to. Mistakes will be made.

The best way to provide instructions to the machine operator is to record the instructions in digital files and then play the appropriate files when they are needed. The operator can continue working while hearing instructions for the next step in the production sequence. Although this is quite simple and straightforward, the machine control must have the ability to not only store and retrieve but also play the audio files.

Automatic Tool Change, Mass Tool Storage

A typical piece of wood furniture cannot be made with a single tool. In fact, some pieces may require twenty, thirty or more different tools to process in a Furniture Fabrication Machine. To produce these parts automatically, the machine must be able to not only change tools automatically but also select from a large source of different tooling.

Many CNC routers offer automatic tool changers but most of these are limited to six or eight tools. Six or eight tools will actually produce a wide variety of furniture, however to produce some of the more complex pieces, many more tools may be required. Systems that offer fifty to a hundred different tools are commercially available and are recommended for truly flexible Furniture Fabrication Machines.

Vertical and Horizontal Tables

A typical CNC router has a horizontal table with the router spindle mounted perpendicular to the table. Parts are mounted to the table and a variety of machining is accomplished. It is in this orientation that most of the machining work will be done.

At times, however, work must be done to the edge of the part. The edge may be edge drilled or dovetails cut. The typical method of accomplishing this work is to use horizontal drills and/or horizontal router spindles. The horizontal orientation allows the tool to address the part edge properly.

The problem with these horizontal tools is that it is virtually impossible to provide tool change capability. This can limit the amount of edge work that can be done on a piece of furniture. This limitation can become a problem in Furniture Fabrication.

Another approach is to turn the part on edge and use the normal vertical tooling to perform the edge work. To do this, the part must be mounted off the side of the table with the edge facing up and located just above the standard worktable. A vertical table attached perpendicular to the standard horizontal table simplifies mounting parts for edge work.

The ability to mount parts vertically as well as horizontally is important to any serious Furniture Fabrication effort.

Measurement Sensor and Decision Making Capability

For a Furniture Fabrication Cell to operate properly it must be able to detect and handle normal variations in the production process. For example, in cutting a long French dovetail, the depth of the dovetail from the upper surface is critical. The machine cut, however, references position from the machine table. Any variation in the thickness of the panel being cut will result in a variation in the depth of the dovetail.

With a position sensor, the actual front surface of each panel can be measured and the program depth adjusted for the exact size of that panel. Normal variations flow through without disrupting the process or requiring exacting thickness tolerances. At the same time, if the variation is beyond an acceptable level the control can alert the operator and stop program execution until a proper blank is loaded.

The position sensor could also be used to check the location of the edge of the part blank to make certain that the correct blank was loaded. The number of uses of a depth sensor is substantial and its use may be critical to certain processes.

For the position sensor to work, not only must it be mounted to the machine but it must be able to interact with the CNC control. It must be able to feed the position information to the control and the control must be able to process this information and integrate it with the production cycle.

The Ability to Carve

Much of the furniture today, especially the higher quality pieces have some carvings. Some furniture has a substantial amount of carving. The ability to do this wood carving on the machine is important to a Furniture Fabrication Cell.

In order to perform wood carving, the machine control must have the ability to store very large programs, must be able to execute these programs quickly and must be able to do this with little or no lag error. The technology behind these requirements is discussed in detail in Chapter 8.

Few CNC controls today have this capability. For a Furniture Fabrication Machine you must make certain that the control selected is one of the few that does.

All of the features required for a Furniture Fabrication Machine are currently available from at least one source. Thermwood Corporation has created Furniture Fabrication Cells with all the features listed above and has demonstrated these at trade shows. One of these cells produces a carved French Provincial wall table from solid cherry. The second produces a reproduction of the classic Newport Knee Chest from solid walnut including dovetail drawers and shell carvings. The third cell reproduces a hand made solid cherry rocking chair including accurately reproducing the small variations indicative of a hand made product.

These demonstrations have clearly shown that the concept is valid and that the economics are real. With the advancing control technology and a desire to move in this direction, it will not be too long before variations of the Furniture Fabrication Machine are available from other sources as well. From the current perspective, if the furniture industry takes a careful look at these ideas, the Furniture Fabrication Cell may very well be the future of furniture production.

Trying to forecast how Furniture Fabrication Cells will evolve is somewhat difficult because it depends on which directions the industry takes when adopting the new technology. Like the plastic molding plant, the new furniture plant will be made up of a multitude of cells each producing a particular piece of furniture.

Higher volume pieces will have more machines devoted to them. Lower volume products will have fewer machines producing them.

The production mix will be changed by switching some machines from one product to another. Multi-shift operations will likely be more common. Most of the skill required is in the equipment. Without the need to track inventory movement and check part set-ups, management will be much easier on the off-shifts.

This trend toward multi-shifts can already be seen in router carvers. These are CNC routers specially set-up to produce wood carvings. As with the Furniture Fabrication Cell, most of the skill is in the equipment. The operator must know something about the operation of the machine but does not need any special skill. It is common, even today to operate these machine twenty-four hours a day and sometimes seven days a week. At these production rates machine and plant overhead costs per part are one third of what they are on a single shift operation.

The Furniture Fabrication Cell does not perform every operation in the factory. The raw stock must be prepared for processing by the cell. For most parts this means thickness planning and belt sanding. In most cases, however, the blank need not be accurately sized. If the part is to be carved, only one surface needs to be planed with the others left rough. It is a good idea to define all final part dimensions in the cell. Final dimensions are then totally dependent on machine tolerances and not on set-up accuracy on one machine or another. In fact, common blanks can be used for different parts that are generally close to the same size. Long feed stock can be used to produce small parts such as braces or glue blocks.

This "loose" need for feed stock can eliminate some of the steps commonly used today in preparing parts for processing on a CNC router. This means fewer steps to manage and slightly lower costs.

Tooling macros will be used to define tool locations and fixture macros will be used to define fixture locations. (macros are discussed in detail in the control section of Chapter 8). In this way, a common set of programs can be used to produce a piece of furniture on any number of machines without the need to very accurately adjust either tooling or fixture positions. We discussed the theory behind tooling macros in the section on zero-set-up. Those same ideas can be applied to the fixture also.

The machine will likely be connected to a network. This will allow them to quickly and easily exchange programs. It will also allow free E-mail communications throughout the network including each of the cells. High-end controls today offer an event file. The control time stamps everything that occurs and puts the information into a file. This file can be accessed at anytime through the network. This access occurs in the background without the cell operator's assistance.

Once this information is gathered, a report can be generated showing the exact status of the entire factory at any time. At the touch of a button you can see exactly how many pieces have been produced, how far along current production has progressed and the current production rate. This information can even be accessed from home through a modem connection to the network server. This can be very helpful for multi-shift operations.

This network technology is here today, it is not science fiction. It has been shipping on CNC routers for years. It is neither difficult nor expensive. Until now, however, numbers showing the production of parts are not very meaningful. You can generate a lot of data but it is difficult to get any real useful information from the data. It is all but impossible to determine the impact of variation in the production of individual components and the effect they will have on finished product production.

With the Furniture Fabrication Cell, however, the data shows you the number of completed saleable products that have been built. This is important information and is easy to understand.

The general level of in-process inventory in the factory should be reduced. An inventory of pre-processed material is required in front of the fabrication cells. An inventory of assembled furniture may be required to stage before the finishing process, depending on the number of unique finishes being applied. Finishing lines that can apply several different finish schedules may reduce or even eliminate this inventory requirement.

Also, if the factory is operated on a multi-shift basis, the floor space requirement per unit of production will also be reduced. This means you can produce more product in smaller factories.

Fewer production employees should be required to produce furniture, perhaps substantially fewer than is currently required. Most material handling and machine set-up labor has been eliminated by the basic production structure. This can be very significant as factory labor shortages continue to get worse. Since the labor requirement is so low in this type of operation, it should be possible to pay a higher wage scale attracting new and more skilled workers.

The Furniture Fabricating Cell operates differently than traditional CNC routers. The cell consists of a highly flexible CNC router, complex clamping and hold-down fixtures and manual support equipment. Support equipment includes sanders, assembly tools and fixtures and other simple tools and machines.

The idea behind the Furniture Fabrication Cell is that the cell and a single operator work together to build a complete piece of furniture. Certain parts of the cycle on the CNC router can be lengthy. In these cases the machine operates automatically leaving the cell operator time to perform secondary operations and assemble the parts.

The technology that we have been discussing is technology that has already been applied in real life Fabrication Cells. As more and different types of furniture are built using this concept, more ideas and techniques will certainly develop. Even now, at the early stages of this technology the cell has shown its ability to produce a variety of products.

The first thing to accept is that a Furniture Fabrication Cell is not a CNC router. Certain operating methods have grown up around the CNC router. These will generally be used when the router is part of a Furniture Fabrication Cell, however, other techniques will also be needed.

The current view of a CNC router is a machine where you load a part, the machine processes the part and then you unload the part. In a fabrication cell, the machine may automatically configure itself as a simple manual machine, a horizontal boring machine for example. The operator will then use it as a horizontal boring machine, loading the part, activating the machine to drill the holes and then removing the part. It could be used in a similar fashion as a chop saw or other simple machine.

Now let us examine the economics of a Furniture Fabrication Cell. The same formulas we have used in the first part of this book also apply here. The differences in how they are applied, however, substantially influence the results.

The first thing to recognize is that unlike all earlier examples, the result of the operation of a Furniture Fabrication Cell is a complete, ASSEMBLED piece of furniture. All past calculations simply calculated the cost of manufacturing a part. That cost did not include final assembly into a finished piece of furniture.

Performing a complete theoretical cost comparison of the cost of manufacturing a piece of furniture using a Fabrication Cell versus any of the more traditional methods will be quite involved. To calculate the traditional manufacturing cost, you must perform the standard cost calculation on each part of the finished piece of furniture. Then you must calculate the cost transporting these parts to the assembly area and assembling them into a finished product.

One good way of performing this calculation for final assembly is to consider the assembly process to be another production center and use the standard formulas. Any equipment costs are treated as the machine cost. Inventory carrying costs and floor space costs are calculated in the normal manner, except, the value of the inventory is now the machined cost of the various components not the raw material cost. Since each part has already had value added to it in the form of machine cost, labor and overhead, it must be valued at the higher level.

The cost of manufacturing using the Fabrication cell is actually quite straightforward to calculate. You have a single production center with inventory in front of it and a complete assembled piece of furniture as the result. The front end inventory and the floor space it occupies will be greater than a typical production center since raw material for every part of the finished piece must be available to the Fabrication Cell.

We are not going to perform specific Fabrication Cell calculations in this book because the actual manufacturing time for a specific piece of furniture and the value of that piece vary too greatly. Any single example we use will be misleading. Instead, we will analyze the differences between traditional manufacturing methods and the Furniture Fabrication Cell. From this analysis, we can get a reasonably accurate picture of the economics of a Fabrication Cell. Each manufacturer, of course, can analyze their own specific case once they know the cycle time and the value of the final product.

The first thing to recognize is that the inventory level required for a Fabrication Cell, although higher than a single production center, will be lower than the overall inventory level in a traditional manufacturing arrangement. In a traditional arrangement inventory and floor space is required in front of every machine in the production process as well as in front of the final assembly process. Each individual component must be processed through at least one, and generally several machines. Each of these machines must therefore have an inventory of material in front of it. Because batch sizes tend to be smaller today, each production center typically has several batches of different components waiting to be processed. As the components move through the factory they gain value and therefore the cost of carrying this inventory increases as they move toward final assembly.

Up to this point, we have ignored this factor, however, in some instances it can have a significant influence on the final cost. It certainly impacts the amount of investment required to operate the factory.

In order to assure accurate assembly of the finished product, every dimension required for assembly should be machined in the Fabrication Cell. For example, the planed thickness of a panel will not be defined in the cell, however, all edges of the panel as well as any interior dimensions should be machined in the cell. When this occurs, however, a sensor on the machine should measure the exact planed thickness of the panel and make any adjustments to the program that might be required. This means that normal tolerances can be handled easily and in many cases the raw material coming to the cell need not be dimensioned accurately. In fact there is no reason to machine the edges of the raw material prior to entering the cell. A part that will be carved in the cell need only be planed on one surface since the other surface will be defined by the carving process.

The result is that although there is more raw material in front of a Fabrication Cell than would be typical of a traditional production center, that raw material is in its lowest cost state. In the

Fabrication Cell, as soon as the component begins to take on value it is assembled into a finished product. It does not sit around the factory as in-process inventory.

It is quite easy to see that a factory consisting of Furniture Fabrication Cells can operate with a lower level of in-process inventory than a typical furniture factory today. The actual level of inventory savings depends on many factors including how efficient current operations are. Because of the fundamental difference in how the two systems operate, however, it is difficult to imagine an instance where the fabrication cell would not have an advantage in inventory cost.

There is another advantage to machining and then immediately assembling the product. Wood is not a stable material. With changes in humidity, wood can change dimension. A part that is machined accurately today may not fit properly a few days from now. To allow for this, additional clearance may need to be machined into the component providing a less than a perfect fit. The entire problem must be dealt with in a traditional factory.

This problem does not exist in a Fabrication Cell. As soon as the part is machined it is assembled. At that point dimensional accuracy should be very good. Should a machining error occur, it will be discovered after one part. It simply won't fit. At that point, you have scrapped one part and the problem can be corrected. If a machining error occurs in a traditional manufacturing environment it is likely that the entire batch will be scrapped.

There are some functions that the Fabrication Cell totally eliminates. Material handling between production centers is totally eliminated, as is the cost of tracking that inventory. This can eliminate a significant cost. Also, the labor used to operate the machine is also used to sand and assemble the finished product. This should also result in lower overall labor requirements.

The Fabrication Cell also eliminates virtually all machine set-up labor. Since the Fabrication Cell is generally dedicated to a specific end product, set-up of a Fabrication Cell occurs very infrequently. Set-up of machines in a traditional factory may occupy a significant percent of the total machining labor. Again, this can be a significant savings.

Elimination of set-up scrap is another major difference between a Fabrication Cell and traditional manufacturing. In traditional manufacturing, each time a machine is set-up for a new part, a test part is run. In many instances this part is scrapped, the machine adjusted and another test part run. This may also be scrapped. After a few parts, the set-up is correct and the batch is processed. The cost of scrapping a few parts at each machine can be significant, especially when batch sizes are small.

If it requires two test parts for each production center and a part must be processed through four production centers, you will scrap eight parts. For a thousand-part run, this is less than one percent and can be tolerated. For a hundred-part run this is eight percent. Eight percent of the material cost of a production run is a significant cost.

There is another practice of a traditional factory that does not exist in the Fabrication Cell. For each batch of parts, a few extra parts are processed. Since you are not quite sure how many parts will be scrapped in set-up or from other causes, it is common to add enough extra parts to the batch to make certain that you do not run short. Should you run short at final assembly you are faced with a difficult decision. Either short the final assembly or set-up each of the machines to produce just a few parts at a very high cost.

A few extra parts are not a problem if they are used on the next production run for this product. Unfortunately, the time and complexity of keeping track of just a few parts for the next time is too much for most companies. The most common practice is to simply discard the extra pieces.

The Fabrication Cell does not require set-up adjustments for individual parts. In most cases, the cell will be dedicated to a single piece of furniture. It must be set up for that piece, however, within that set-up every part required for that piece of furniture can be loaded and run with no additional set-up. Should the operator damage or scrap a part in the assembly process, it is a simple matter to process just one replacement part. Test parts are not needed and extra safety parts are not needed. These facts further enhance the economic benefits of the Furniture Fabrication Cell.

The Furniture Fabrication Cell, as we are proposing it here, includes a sophisticated CNC router, a rather complex set of programs and fixtures and some means of guiding the operator through the rather long production cycle. The easiest guide to use is voice instructions executed as part of the CNC program. These instructions are actually recorded voice instructions, played back to the operator instructing him or her what they should do next and perhaps how to do it.

If you examine the cell described here you quickly see that the skill is in the machine. It requires a certain level of technical skill to set up and program the cell, however, it does not require a particularly high skill level to actually run the cell. Very little judgment and very little management involvement is required to run the cell.

This means that it is relatively simple to run a Furniture Fabrication Cell on a multi-shift basis. Most furniture factories operate on a single shift. Most that have attempted multi-shift operation have discovered that trying to manage the off shifts was more than they were capable of. The problems associated with the off shifts more than offset any savings that might be achieved.

With the Furniture Fabrication Cell, however, multi-shift operation makes perfect sense. Since the skill is in the machine and very little judgment or management input is required, there are few problems to interfere with the potential savings.

The two major benefits of multi-shift operation are lower per hour machine costs and higher production capacity for the machine investment. As we saw earlier, one major factor in calculating per hour machine cost is machine utilization. The more hours per year a machine is used, the lower the per hour cost.

A Fabrication Cell should have a very high utilization rate since it is the only production machine. Unlike other machines that may only be needed part of the time for the production levels required, a Furniture Fabrication Cell will generally be utilized all the time since it is the only production machine. Because of its ease of use it is very likely that it will be operated on a multi-shift basis which further reduces cost.

The plastics molding industry has a similar situation. The major production machine in a plastics factory is an injection molding machine. This machine is expensive and, like the Fabrication Cell, the skill is in the machine. Faced with the same situation, the plastics industry almost universally operates three shifts a day.

As this book is being written, only demonstration Furniture Fabrication Cells have operated. These have demonstrated that all the technologies required to make the cell function are commercially available. These have produced complex high-end all wood furniture and the economics of this type of production can be estimated fairly accurately. These examples show that, at least in this instance, the Fabrication Cell produces furniture at a reduced cost. The logic presented here supports the idea that the Fabrication Cell will also produce other types of furniture at different price points and at a lower manufacturing cost than is common today.

Some of the features and advantages of a Furniture Fabrication Cell are as follows:

Lower labor requirements, the machine operator also sands and assembles the finished piece of furniture

Audio guide, the machine control "talks" the operator through the production and assembly process (patent pending)

Lower inventory requirements, no need for stacks of parts in front of a multitude of woodworking machines

Less material handling, no need to move parts from department to department

Fewer employees required for production, since individual departments, machine set-up and material handling have been eliminated, so has the associated labor

Less mill processing, many times rough lumber or material planed on one side can be processed by the cell

Dimensionally stable parts, since parts are assembled right after machining, they do not have time to gain or lose moisture and change dimensions. They fit.

Tool management, the control keeps track of the use of each tool and alerts the operator when a tool reaches the end of its useful life

Maintenance clock, the control keeps track of the use of each part of the machine and alerts the operator only when lubrication or routine maintenance is absolutely necessary

Production tracking, the exact status and production completed by each cell can be monitored through a network

Higher quality end product, since all parts are produced on one machine with no need for set-up or dimension adjustments, part accuracy is very high and reject rates very low

No delays for QC set-up checks, since traditional machine set-up does not exist, the need to have QC check and sign-off the set-up is no longer necessary

Easy replacement part production, any part being produced by the cell can be made at any time without disrupting the current production cycle. Parts damaged in assembly can be quickly and easily replaced

Simplified scheduling and production control, controlling the output of a cell is much simpler than controlling the flow through dozens of machines and departments

Single source responsibility, a single operator is responsible for the output of a cell so problems can be quickly isolated and corrected

Less scrap potential, a material or programming error will be found after a single cycle, not after an entire batch has been scrapped

Multi-shift potential, since operation of the cell is straightforward requiring little management input, it is practical to operate on more than one shift reducing machinery and overhead costs

High machine utilization rate, since the cell is the entire production process, it is operating most of the time, unlike traditional machines that may spend 80 or 90% of the time either idle or being set-up

Lower floor space requirement, since the cell replaces many traditional machines and the in-process inventory in front of them, the overall factory floor space requirements are substantially less

Eliminate set-up scrap and "safety" parts, traditional machines may scrap one or two parts during each set-up and it is common to produce several extra parts "just in case". With the Fabrication Cell these are no longer necessary so costs are lower

Once developed, programs can be moved from one cell to another without the need for reposting, macros in each machine define the physical characteristics, tooling and fixture location so programs don't need to, they simply call the macros

Chapter 8

CNC Router Design

Chapter 8

CNC Router Design

The CNC router will be the major factor in a Furniture Fabrication Cell. Because companies that adopt this concept will be absolutely relying on CNC routers for their production, it is important that they understand some of the underlying technology.

The CNC router market is highly competitive. There are literally dozens of companies struggling to sell their products. Many of these companies attempt to convince the customer that their machine is better than their competition. They cite engineering features claiming that their design is acknowledged as better. Or, they simply state that they have a feature, weight for example and hope that the customer simply assumes that the more weight the better.

Some companies actually present engineering facts and use these to prove that their design is better. In some of these cases, the facts are true but, other factors may actually be more important. In the end, this is a confusing collage of conflicting claims that few customers can make sense of.

In this chapter we will try and make some sense of the engineering and technology surrounding CNC routers. Unfortunately, presenting this information has one major drawback. It may cause some to believe that they are qualified to judge a CNC router on technical grounds.

Machine tool design is a highly complex science. It is a balancing act. There is no accepted, proper way to design a machine tool. Every decision, every component is a compromise. Each time you select a direction to achieve some benefit, you also give up other benefits and capability. In no area of machine design can you gain something without giving up something else.

From this perspective, judging machine design is trying to determine which of the available technologies or design alternatives the machine designer chose. These features also work or blend together. A series of design directions that each taken alone might not be the best could, working together, provide excellent results. This makes judging a particular machine design by examining the engineering specifications a very difficult task. It is a little like trying to guess what a meal will taste like by looking at the recipe. You may get an idea, but the real test is in the tasting. The fact is that there are probably less than a dozen people in the entire United States that are truly able to judge a machine from its basic design. It is very likely that none of these people work in the furniture industry.

The only really accurate way to judge a machine is to judge the results. How well does the machine actually perform its tasks? How good is the quality of the product it produces? How easy is it to use? How well does it hold up in production? How reliable is it? How long does it last? How easy is it to upgrade or change? What does it cost?

It is safe to assume that if a machine scores well on these questions it is a good design. If it does not, it is not a good design. It is possible for each of us to rather accurately judge the overall design quality of a machine by examining how well it actually works in similar production.

When you focus on the engineering detail of a machine design you are in fact saying "I can tell how well a machine will perform better by looking at the design than by looking at how it actually performs". When we put it this way, it sort of looks ridiculous, yet that is exactly how many companies try and sell their machines and how many companies buy their machines.

Now that we understand this, it can still be useful to understand basic CNC router design so that we understand the decisions that our machine designer made.

We must now understand that a CNC router is not a modified metalworking machine. Many in the furniture industry believe that metalworking machines are much more advanced and much more sophisticated than CNC routers. The opposite is actually true. Certainly the design demands of a woodworking machine are much more difficult to achieve than a metalworking machine.

Metalworking machines are designed to achieve very tight accuracy tolerances but at a very slow feed speed, typically 1/10 to 1/100 of that required by a woodworking machine. This difference in operating speed speaks to the core of differences in design between metalworking machines and woodworking machines.

As speeds increase, the dynamics of everything come into play. It is substantially more difficult to achieve five or ten thousandths of an inch accuracy operating at 100 or 150 inches per minute than to achieve a half thousandth tolerance at 10 inches per minute. Because of its higher speed, a woodworking machine will travel 10 to 100 times farther during its operating life than a metalworking machine. A combination of weight, slides and friction that offers a more than adequate life for slow moving metalworking applications might prove to have only one tenth to one one-hundredth the life needed for a woodworking application.

In metalworking, the control is simply cooled with a fan and a coarse filter. Metal chips are rather large in size. The factory air might have coolant or oil suspended in it but there is little danger of it condensing on the control components. In a woodworking environment the air is filled with suspended particles of sawdust. These come in all sizes from very coarse to extremely fine. If these particles are allowed to enter the control enclosure they will be deposited on the control components. This will cause few problems in the first couple of years but after five or six years problems can be severe enough to consider scrapping out the entire machine. Again, a design decision that is more than adequate for metalworking doesn't work well in woodworking.

The design decisions that are made in designing a metalworking machine cannot be the same as those made in designing a woodworking machine. The requirements are vastly different and require a fundamentally different design. If you try and judge a CNC router design by using criteria from the metalworking industry you will likely end up with totally misleading results.

In the remainder of this chapter we will focus on specific requirements of the wood industry and compare the different ways these needs can be met.

Let us start with the basic machine configuration. CNC routers have been built in four different configurations over the years. Today, two of these dominate the machine offerings. Each of these configurations can work equally well. Those companies that claim one is better than another are simply wrong. Each does have strong and weak points, however, if properly engineered each will produce high quality production.

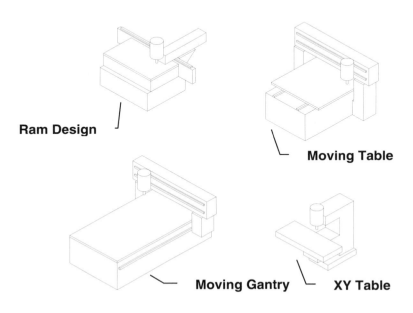

Ram Design

Moving Table

Moving Gantry   **XY Table**

Common CNC Router Configurations

This can be very confusing if you listen to the desperate claims of some machine manufacturers that claim that only one design will do your job. By coincidence this is the only design they build. These people will point out factors that must be taken into account when a configuration is chosen and show that it makes a particular configuration slow, inaccurate or unstable. The truth is that none of the configurations will work properly if they are designed incorrectly. The converse is also true, all will work very well if they are properly engineered. The basic configuration you select should be based on other factors than the belief that one is inherently better than another.

The first NC routers were a ram design. A tool carriage ran left and right on a set of rails located directly behind the worktable. The worktable was about two feet wide and eight to ten feet long.

The operator stood with the ten-foot dimension to his left and right. A ram type structure was mounted to the carriage so that it could move from the back of the table, two-feet to the front of the table. The head could then cover the entire table, front to back and left to right.

This configuration has one major advantage. It is easy to load and unload. The table is suspended in front of the operator and all of the operating mechanism is located behind the table. Every part of the two-foot wide table can be easily reached.

Its major disadvantage is the table width. A part over two feet wide cannot be completely machined, although some companies machine wide parts by machining as much of the part as possible and then turning the part around to machine the other side. This type of machine has been built with a wider table, however, since the ram structure is suspended from only one side, developing a structure that remains rigid becomes quite difficult. In general this is an area where you try and create a very rigid but lightweight structure.

Today, the ram style machine is commonly used for point-to-point machining centers but is seldom used for the somewhat more demanding CNC router applications.

Another machine style that is seldom used is the X-Y table. In this design, a table that moves in both right and left and front to back is mounted under a spindle that moves up and down. The first of these machines was actually a pin router with an X-Y table mounted to it.

It is quite easy to get a very rigid machine using this design, however, from a practical standpoint it is limited to rather small table sizes. The spindle must be attached to the machine base by an upright column. The distance from the column to the spindle defines the maximum table width and this distance cannot be too large without making the overall machine structure impractical.

The final two machine configurations, the fixed table/moving gantry and the moving table/fixed gantry designs are the most common in industry today. Properly applied each design produces essentially the same results but the design requirements for each are quite different.

The moving table machine is more common than the fixed table machine, not because it is inherently more stable as some manufacturers might have you believe. Instead it is more common because of a control system limitation.

To understand this, we must understand how modern machines achieve their accuracy. A ball screw and nut drive most machine axes. The nut is actually a bearing that turns on the screw with very little friction. The ball nut is mounted to the part of the machine that is to move and the screw is mounted to the base. As the screw turns, it moves the ball nut and the axis it is connected to.

This is simple enough until you think about accuracy. To accurately position the nut, the screw must be very accurate. If there is any error, called pitch error, in the screw the position that the control thinks the nut is at and its actual position will be different. So how do we get an accurate screw?

Screws are made using two different processes. The first is the rolled ball screw where the ball tracks are rolled into the screw shaft using a special machine. This produces a high quality screw but, because of the nature of the rolling process, one that is susceptible to pitch error. Even a high quality rolled ball screw can have a pitch error of .010 to .015 inch per foot of length. This means a ten-foot screw could be off by .150 inch or over an eighth of an inch. This is outside a practical tolerance for woodworking.

The second type of screw is the ground lead screw. In a ground lead screw the track is rolled or machined into the rod and then precision ground to a high level of accuracy. A ground lead screw can be manufactured with a tolerance of only a few thousandths of an inch per foot instead of ten to fifteen thousandths per foot for a rolled lead screw.

There are two problems with this. First it is very very expensive. A ground lead screw can cost thousands and thousands of dollars. This might be alright if it were very accurate but with only a few thousandths of an inch error per foot the axis can still be off twenty to thirty thousandths over ten feet. While this may be acceptable for most applications, it is still undesirable especially when you consider the money invested.

The answer to this problem has come from the control system manufacturers. The only problem with a rolled lead screw is that when the control thinks the axis is in one position it is actually in a slightly different position depending on the pitch error of the screw. If the control knew the exact pitch error of the screw, it could allow for that error when positioning the axis, achieving accuracy well beyond the accuracy of the screw.

The feature that performs this correction is called lead screw compensation. The control system maintains a lead screw compensation table that is actually a map of the differences between where the control thinks the axis is and where it actually is. This table is created after the machine is built by moving through the entire range of motion and comparing the actual position of each axis with the theoretical position. The most accurate way to measure the actual position is by using a laser interferometer. This is a measurement device that can measure to an accuracy in the millionths of an inch over large distances. This process is so sensitive that factors such as temperature, humidity and barometric pressure must be taken into account because they slightly affect the speed of light, which can affect measurements this small.

Lead screw compensation tables can also be created using a reference screw. This is either a very accurate screw or one that has been previously mapped using the laser. This process is normally done to the screw before it is assembled to the machine and has the disadvantage of only allowing for lead screw error. When the table is created on the finished machine it compensates for any machine factor that might affect accuracy. After having said all this, the machine accuracy that results from either of these practices is normally more than enough for any furniture application.

Each control system manufacturer offers a different number of compensation points per axis. Some offer a couple of hundred for the entire machine while others offer thousands per axis. The closer the compensation points are to each other the more accurately the screw is mapped but the harder the control must work to keep track of actual position.

The result of all of this is that using a rolled ball screw and lead screw compensation table we can achieve positioning accuracy that is much better than a much more expensive ground lead screw without compensation.

At times you may see someone using both a ground lead screw and a lead screw compensation table. Does this give even more accurate results as the manufacturer will likely claim? Actually no. Some older and some lower cost CNC controls limit the amount of compensation that can be entered into the compensation table. By limiting the size of the number, calculations can be performed using fewer bits. This reduces both cost and complexity. The practical result is that many times a rolled lead screw cannot be properly mapped within the limits of the control. The next best thing is to use a ground lead screw, however, is it not necessary to make the screw as accurate as possible. It is only necessary to make the screw accurate enough to fit within the mapping limits of the control. This can be much less expensive than a highly accurate ground lead screw. In general however, a ground lead screw is overkill for wood machining applications and results in a machine that is substantially more expensive, without offering any measurable benefit for the extra cost.

This is one of those engineering decisions that must be made. Do I use a more capable but more expensive control and lower cost rolled lead screws, or do I use a low cost control but somewhat more expensive ground lead screws? The positioning results of both will be essentially the same.

Now that we understand lead screw compensation, let us turn back to machine configuration. A moving table machine has a single lead screw moving the head back and forth on the gantry and a single screw moving the table front to back. This is a straightforward arrangement.

A fixed table machine has the moving gantry mounted to a rail located on either side of the table. This gantry is normally driven by a lead screw along each rail. One lead screw moves the head back and forth on the gantry but it requires two lead screws to move the gantry. This is where it gets a little tricky.

Movement of the gantry is a single axis. This single axis, however, must drive two servomotors, not one. Each servomotor drives a lead screw. The chances of the two lead screws being exactly matched are virtually zero so a single compensation table won't work. Each screw must have its own independent compensation table. As you can see this can get quite complicated.

Control system manufacturers have created a package to address this requirement called "gantry software". This configuration is commonly used on multi-million dollar aerospace machine tools so the control manufacturers haven't been shy about its price. It is not uncommon for gantry software to double the cost of a control.

So, the fixed table machine requires one extra servomotor and drive, and requires gantry software making it more expensive. It is easy to understand why the moving table has become the most popular design.

There have been several attempts to work around these areas. The most direct is to use a single drive motor running two screws through a jack shaft, belts, or the like. The biggest concern with this arrangement is to determine how the differences in pitch error between the two screws has been handled. It is possible to select and match screws within a reasonable tolerance but this is a time consuming and difficult task. When this is done, the compensation table should be the average of the pitch error of the two screws making each side off by half the difference.

It is also difficult to design a drive system to connect the two screws that provides a solid drive with no lash.

Another method that is starting to be used in fixed table designs is to cantilever the table, supporting it at each end and then connecting the legs of the gantry underneath the table. The gantry is then driven by a single screw in the middle, underneath the table eliminating the need for gantry software.

The only potential problem with this arrangement is that it is more difficult to achieve a rigid structure. There is a tendency for the gantry to skew when a heavy cut is taken at the edge of the table. The bearing and rail structure must be substantially stiffer for this arrangement to work equally well. Achieving this level of stiffness will add cost to the machine and at some point it makes more sense to go back and drive the gantry from both sides.

When talking to a new machine manufacturer make certain that they are aware of, and address the lead screw compensation issue. There are companies that simply ignore this and let the customer live with the results. In some cases they do this where the control is more than capable of providing the compensation function.

The moving table machine design and the moving gantry machine design achieve essentially the same results if both are equally well engineered. The biggest difference between the two designs is that for equal table size, the moving table design requires about twice the floor space. The fixed table is made up of the table and enough area around the table for the gantry to ride. The moving table machine needs enough room for the table to move its entire length requiring at least twice the space.

There are some other differences between the two designs that really don't apply to the wood industry. A fixed table machine can generally carry heavier parts than a moving table machine. Table movement must not only move the table but must also move the fixture and workpiece. When the fixture and workpiece weigh thousands of pounds, this can become a problem. In these circumstances it is better to place the fixture and workpiece on a fixed table braced to the floor and move the gantry over the work. Large aerospace machines are always fixed table moving gantry designs. They have large tables and process heavy fixtures and parts.

We have indicated that the design requirements for the two machines are different. One basic difference has to do with rigidity and weight. This is an area that generates huge levels of confusion many times fostered by machine manufacturers trying to justify their own design decisions.

Let us return to fundamentals. The purpose of the machine is to produce accurate, high quality parts. High quality generally means smooth even cuts. It is generally believed that this is achieved by using a rigid, accurate machine and, at least today, this is still true. It very well may not be true in the very near future, however.

There is a great deal of work being done on machines that react to the machining process. High-speed sensors look at the machining process as it is occurring. The instant it sees the machine reacting to the cutting forces it instantly compensates for the machine movement. In theory, the machine could be made of rubber and still machine very accurate parts. Once this is achieved, machine structure and rigidity will no longer be important. Today, the machine must be more accurate than the most accurate part you want to make with it. In the near future, machines may be able to make parts that are more accurate than the machines they are made on.

An important point is that, at least today, we are interested in machine rigidity. Not mass, not weight, but rigidity. They are not the same thing.

In the past, in the metalworking industry, rigidity was achieved by adding mass. One could accurately assume that the heavier the machine the more rigid the machine. This is no longer true. We are not now in the past and we are not in the metalworking industry, so these concepts may not work for us. In fact applying outdated thinking to a modern machine may result in a machine that neither performs well nor lasts very long.

Ultimately we want a machine that will produce a good quality part and a machine that will last a long time. With today's technology it requires a rigid machine to produce a good part. The machine rigidity resists the cutting forces to achieve the cut path desired.

The practice of achieving rigidity through mass that was common in the metalworking industry does not work as well in the wood industry. While you can develop a very rigid machine by making it very massive, this approach sacrifices other requirements. Some of these requirements exist in wood but don't exist in metal.

Cycle times in metalworking are generally fairly long with cycles of ten minutes to an hour being common. Cycle times in woodworking are much shorter. Feed speeds in the metalworking industry are relatively slow while feed speeds in woodworking are fast. Cycle times are heavily influenced by the acceleration and deceleration rates of the machine. The acceleration rate, that is, how quickly you can reach top speed and the deceleration rate, how quickly you can stop, are key factors when feed speeds are high but are much less important at low feed speeds.

The engineering choices made when designing a metalworking machine tend to favor achieving rigidity by adding mass. As a machine becomes more massive, it becomes more difficult to move. It requires more power from the drives and places more loads on the slides and drives. It is more difficult to accelerate and decelerate a massive machine.

These disadvantages are relatively minor in a metalworking machine since neither acceleration nor high top speeds are important. In a woodworking application, however, both acceleration and top speed are very important. The disadvantages of achieving rigidity by simply making the machine very massive also make it less desirable for woodworking applications.

Designing a machine for woodworking applications requires developing a rigid structure that is still light enough to achieve proper accelerations and decelerations. This is a much more difficult task than faced by the metalworking machine designer.

We are not going to endorse any specific method of achieving the design goals. Each machine designer has his or her own approach. Some simply opt for a massive machine, install equally massive drives and install oversized rails and drive screws to handle the higher loads and simply live with the higher costs. Others create a simple light structure and tolerate a lower level of rigidity. Still others use computer aided stress and vibration analysis to develop structures that are both rigid and light. There are many variations between these approaches.

It is virtually impossible to try and second-guess the design approach for a machine tool. The only way to tell if a machine design is any good is to watch it operate. Compare cycle times, product quality and machine price and determine from these if the machine is right for your application.

Certain companies in the industry promote the idea that only with a massive machine can you achieve the results you want. They claim that cast iron is superior to other materials for machine tool structures. As we have already shown, neither of these statements is absolutely true.

There is no one superior material. Each material has properties that help and other properties that hurt your design. Cast iron provides mass and rigidity but it is not a particularly strong material and it is subject to cracking with shock loads. Steel provides very high strength and rigidity but must be fabricated into a structure rather than being cast like cast iron or aluminum. Aluminum is rigid and lightweight but has lower yield point than steel or cast iron. Each material has its place in a machine design and claiming that one material is always superior is irresponsible.

Certain exotic materials such as aluminum honeycomb are many times more rigid pound for pound than steel or cast iron. These materials have been used to produce CNC routers for specialty applications but today they are much too expensive for widespread use.

At this point, we have examined the basic configuration and basic design requirements for a CNC router. You should have a feeling that there are no right answers. This is actually true. The right machine design and the right machine configuration is the one that fits your application the best.

Now, let us turn to the drives, the devices that cause the machine to move. Three different drive motors have been used to power CNC routers, stepping motors, DC servo drives and AC servo drives. Again, each has advantages and disadvantages.

A stepping motor uses a permanent magnet rotor and wire wound stator. The stator is wound so that the motor has a large number of poles, typically 200. These poles are generally arranged in groups of four. When one pole is energized, the rotor will align with that pole and is locked in place. The force that it exerts holding that position is essentially the amount of torque available from the motor.

When an adjacent pole is energized and the current pole turned off, the rotor "steps" over to the new position. This stepping motion between poles is the origin of the stepping motor name.

When the third pole is energized it again moves as with the fourth pole. The next step, or the fifth pole uses the same control pattern as the first pole. As we said earlier, the poles are arranged in groups of four. This is an important concept because it may influence performance and accuracy.

When any particular pole is energized, the rotor is locked in position. Should you exert enough force to rotate the rotor from this locked position it will jump over four poles and align with the fifth pole. The control signals that hold the rotor in position repeat every four poles which means that with any position signal the rotor can be locked in any of 50 positions on a 200 pole motor.

The basis for using a stepping motor to run a machine is to take control of the rotor, use a reference, such as a limit switch to determine exact position and then rotate the motor carefully enough so that you never lose control of the rotor. If you never skip steps but always keep control of the rotor, the computer will always know the current position of the axis. Since no position feedback is used, this is called an "open loop" system. The control commands a motor position and then simply assumes that the machines follows the command.

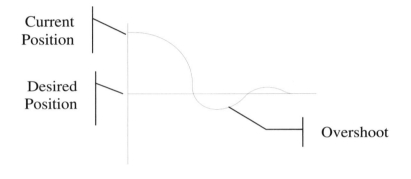

Current
Position

Desired
Position

Overshoot

Stepping Motor Step Overshoot

In theory this sounds quite simple, however, large stepping motors have a characteristic that make controlling them a bit more difficult. Let us examine what happens when you move from one step to another. When the step occurs, the rotor feels a force trying to move it to the next pole. This force causes the rotor to rotate toward the next pole. When it reaches the next pole the rotor is still moving so it tends to move past it or overshoot until the pull of the pole stops its rotation and starts it moving back. When it again reaches the pole it is again moving, this time in the opposite direction and not quite as fast. It again passes the pole, stops and reverses. Thus when the rotor moves from one pole to another it oscillates about the new pole for a fraction of a second until finally comes to a stop. This characteristic can be a problem at certain specific speeds. Let's say the rotor moves past the new pole, reverses and moves past the pole again, back toward the original pole. If, at that very instant another step occurs, the rotor is farther from the new pole than it would normally be. Thus the force on the rotor will be greater and it will oscillate farther to each side of the next pole. If again the next step occurs when the pole is farthest away from the new pole, the overshoot again increases. Within a few steps, the forces become high enough that the rotor skips four poles and the control no longer knows the rotor position.

There are several ways of addressing this problem, but for a stepping motor drive to function properly it must be addressed.

The most fundamental approach is to vary the voltage or power sent to the stepping motor based on rotor rotation speed. If you can reduce the force trying to rotate the rotor you can slow down movement from one pole to the next. The idea is to try and balance the time it takes to move from one pole to the next with the time between steps. If you can do this properly, as the rotor reaches the next pole, the system steps again and there is not enough time to oscillate about each pole.

Although the theory is relatively simple, many factors including machine mass and cutting loads affect rotor rotation time with a fixed voltage. This means any system designed to eliminate oscillation must be a compromise and will not work perfectly under all circumstances.

Another method of controlling stepping motors is called microstepping. Instead of simply energizing each pole, one at a time, the microstepper systematically balances forces between two adjacent poles to carefully rotate the field and thus the rotor. This system does pretty well eliminate oscillation but because much of the time the rotor is being acted on by two opposing poles, overall torque may be reduced.

Stepping Motor and Viscous Dampener

Another device that can help eliminate oscillation is a viscous dampener. This is a machined canister connected to the rotor shaft of the motor. Inside the canister is a mass, which is free to rotate with only a few thousands of an inch clearance from the canister walls. This space is filled with a highly viscous fluid. This arrangement then provides a large amount of rotary dampening primarily in the speed range where oscillation occurs.

Stepping motors were used in early CNC routers primarily because they were substantially lower cost than other drives at the time. Properly engineered, they perform well in less demanding applications. Again, when properly engineered the open loop feature was not a significant problem although, in practice, it was a good idea to perform the reference procedure often.

As the cost of DC servo drives and AC servo drives came down, stepping motors lost favor. Their greatest advantage, cost, was no longer as significant and the technical effort required to properly apply them was greater than with the alternative drives.

Today, a number of new, low cost machines have again begun using stepping motors. When evaluating these machines make certain that they are engineered properly to take care of oscillation and that they are balanced enough that they do not lose steps when executing a program.

The next most common drive is the DC servo. A DC servomotor is configured with a permanent magnet stator and a wound wire rotor. The permanent magnets making up the stator are attached to the outer case of the motor. A set of carbon brushes transfer power through an armature to the wound stator.

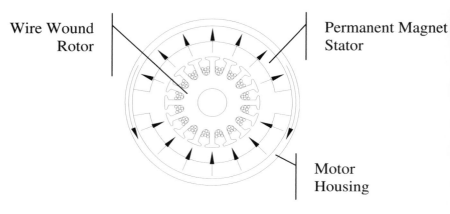

Diagram of DC Servomotor

A position feedback sensor or encoder is attached to the rotor so that as it rotates, a signal is sent to the drive indicating the position of the rotor. When the system is first energized, the axis moves until a switch or other signal determines a reference machine axis position. Once the reference point is achieved, the control keeps track of the rotation of the servomotor through the encoder. This is a closed loop system unlike the stepping motor. Not only does the control dictate the position but it also checks through the encoder to determine whether or not its control signals have been executed.

An axis controlled by a stepping motor is positioned by feeding the proper number of steps to the stepping motor drive. The motor then steps to the correct position. A DC servo works differently.

As we said earlier, the control knows the position of the DC motor rotor by reading the encoder. When the control wants the motor to move, it knows where the motor is currently positioned and where it should be positioned. The difference between these two positions is called an error signal. This error signal is fed to the servo drive, amplified and fed to the servomotor to cause it to turn in the direction needed to eliminate the error signal. As the error signal becomes smaller, the voltage fed to the drive also becomes smaller and motor rotation slows until there is no error signal and the drive is stopped.

Although there is no force on the motor in the stopped position, as soon as you try to rotate the rotor, an error signal is developed, amplified and fed to the servomotor to resist your motion. It is as if the motor is locked in position.

The amount that the error signal is amplified is called the "gain". The servo closure loop generally takes into account other factors than just the error signal to try and obtain better performance. Sometimes the error signal is mathematically integrated over time. This means that the longer an error signal exists for an axis, the harder the motor tries to close the gap.

To obtain motion of the axis, the control continuously redefines the position that the motor should be at. Error signals are developed as the desired position becomes different than the current position forcing the motor to "chase" the point that was programmed.

The greatest advantage that the DC servo system has over the stepping motor is that there is no danger of losing steps. The closed loop nature of the design means that the current position is always known. Acceleration and deceleration in a stepping motor system must be limited to make certain that the holding torque of the motor is never exceeded. Otherwise steps and position would be lost. A DC servomotor does not have that same limitation. The torque available for acceleration and deceleration will be higher.

This higher torque generally means better performance. On most part programs, cutting speeds are defined by the material and cutting tool and are not a machine limitation. The only difference between machines is generally how fast the machine can accelerate to that cutting speed and how quickly it can come to a stop. These factors can substantially impact cycle time, many times more than top speed.

DC servomotors do, however, have problems of their own that must be addressed. The first centers around the fact that an error signal must be present for the system to work. This means that the machine is never at the position it is supposed to be at. It always lags behind the proper position. The distance that it lags behind is called a "lag error". If you think about it you will realize that the faster an axis tries to move the greater the lag error.

Another potential problem occurs when you come to a stop. If the axis you are trying to stop is massive and machine friction too small to stop the axis quickly enough, then the servomotor must stop the axis. It must create force in the direction opposite the movement of the axis. To create this force, however, the axis must drive past the desired position and create an error signal in the opposite direction. The actual position in now leading the desired position. The amount that it leads the desired position is called a "lead error".

Under these circumstances, when the desired position comes to a stop, the axis, which was running ahead of the desired position, will have overshot the stop position. It will need to reverse direction and return to the desired stopping point. If this overshoot occurs while machining an inside corner, a machining defect will result. The only way to address this is to either reduce the mass of the axis, increase the friction so that a lead error does not develop or reduce deceleration so that a lead error does not develop.

Overshoot at part corner

This is prime example of where trying to build a massive machine to achieve high performance doesn't make sense. The mass is the single biggest contributor to degraded performance. I have observed machines in operation where the designer did not take this into account. When cutting square corners, the machine overshot the corner and didn't recover until part way down the next side. It cut a "bubble" where a square corner should have been.

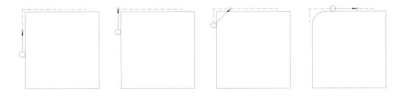

Lag Error Causes Rounded Corner

Another common problem with square corners is rounding the corner. If you think about it, a servo loop is a little like pulling a weight around with a spring. The length of the spring is the lag error and corresponds to the error signal. You trace the desired position with the end you are pulling and the weight follows some distance behind. When you come to a corner, if you do not wait until the error signal becomes zero, you will start pulling the weight sideways before it reaches the corner. Although you traced a perfectly square corner, the weight actually rounded the corner. Many CNC controls actually have a command called Absolute Stop which makes sure that the corner has been properly reached before beginning the next move.

Lead/lag error can also cause problems when you are trying to coordinate more than one axis at a time. Because of lag error, the actual position of an axis is behind the position that was programmed. With a single axis motion this is not much of a problem. Although the position in time is not exactly the same, the path is correct and that is ultimately what you are interested in.

When you try and coordinate the movement of two or more axis simultaneously, you must consider the lag error of each axis independently. The lag errors of each axis must be adjusted so that each axis lag error is the same as all other axes lag error at every speed and every acceleration. This servo tuning procedure is part science and part art.

When properly tuned, the lag errors of all axes balance and the machine travels the programmed path although slightly behind the desired position in time. To properly tune a machine, however, it is generally necessary to try and balance the mass of each axis to try and get the lag error as close to the same mechanically before you try to tune it electronically. Trying to balance a massive axis with a light axis is almost impossible using a conventional servo closure loop.

Just how large are these lag errors? I have worked with an older set of DC drives, a commercial CNC control and a massive machine where lag errors of four to six inches were experienced. The final machine, however, was used in aerospace and could machine very accurate parts.

Generally, the greater the torque available from the servomotors the tighter you can make the servo loop and the lower the lag error. Lighter machines will operate with less lag error than heavy machines.

Recently a new type of servo loop has developed that operates with very little lag error. This system can operate with lag errors of only five or ten thousandths of an inch rather than lag errors measured in inches. This system requires high-speed computer processors in the servo closure loop. These computers generate the error signal, not from the actual error signal but by looking ahead in the program and calculating what the error signal will be at some point in the future. By combining the actual lag error and the anticipated future error, an error signal is generated that anticipates future movement. If you go back to our analogy of pulling a weight with a spring, this system doesn't lead the front end of the spring around the programmed path. Instead, it moves the lead end of the spring around a path calculated to make the weight move on the desired position along the path. This path is generally calculated to operate with a very small lag error because lag errors generally cause fewer machining problems than lead errors.

For this system to work well, however, requires a responsive servomotor with plenty of torque. How do we get more torque from our servomotor?

We could, of course, install a larger servomotor. While this will give us more torque, to obtain that increased torque requires that wire wound rotor be made larger. This larger rotor has more mass which makes it more difficult to accelerate and decelerate. The mass of the motor rotor is the single biggest factor in determining acceleration.

What would happen if we just fed more power into the existing DC motor? Since the power must be transferred to the rotor through the brushes, at some level of power, the brushes will no longer be able to carry the current and will begin to arc. This is obviously the maximum power that can be transferred. If we operate just below this level, however, another problem develops.

As electric power moves through the windings in the rotor, heat is generated. This heat must exit from the rotor across an air gap to the permanent magnet stator, through the magnets to the motor housing and then through the motor housing to the surrounding air. This is a rather long heat path. The efficiency of this heat path determines the maximum average power that a DC servomotor can generate. If the heat being generated cannot be dissipated, the motor will burn up.

To address these problems, a new type of servomotor has become popular today. This motor is commonly called an AC servo. It is also called a brushless DC servo by some companies.

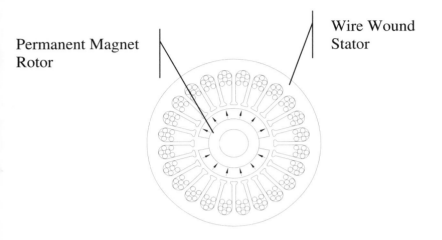

Permanent Magnet
Rotor

Wire Wound
Stator

Diagram of AC Servomotor

This motor is constructed differently from the DC servomotor. In an AC servomotor, the rotor is a permanent magnet and the stator is wire wound. Because there are no wires in the rotor, there is no need for brushes. Commutation is performed electronically by the servo drive rather than being performed by the brushes and commutator.

Lets look at the advantages of this arrangement. First, because there are no brushes to arc, the maximum limit to the power you can feed to the motor is only limited to the power required to melt the wires in the stator. As you can imagine, this is substantially greater than the power you can feed through rotating brushes. The average power that a motor can operate at is also higher. Since the wire windings, which generate the heat, are the stator they are attached directly to the motor housing. Instead of the long heat path of the DC servo motor, the heat from an AC servomotor must only travel from the windings through the motor housing to the outside air.

The result is that in the same frame size, an AC servomotor will provide more power. It can also generate bursts of power well beyond normal as long as the average power is below the design limit. The permanent magnet rotor generally has less mass than a wire wound rotor making acceleration and deceleration faster. Higher end AC servomotors use rare earth magnets that have less mass and can contain higher magnetic fields than iron cores. These provide even higher acceleration deceleration performance.

These are the three most commonly used drive means for CNC routers. In the early days, some CNC routers were hydraulically powered, however, this method is not used today. Each of the methods can work well, subject to their design limitations, provided they are properly engineered. Poorly engineered, all will perform poorly.

Stepping motors were commonly used because of their low cost. Today, however, the high end of the stepping motor technology and the low end of DC servomotor technology have met. Low-end stepping motors that do not address step resonance are generally not suitable for powering CNC routers. DC servomotors have come down in price and, today, these appear to be a better choice for low cost machines.

Pretty well everyone agrees that AC servomotors have the performance edge but they generally cost more. You must make sure that the machine design can take advantage of the higher performance drives. It makes little sense to pay more for drives that do not provide additional machine performance.

Now that we have looked at the drive motors, let's examine exactly how they move the axis. There are several methods that are used to convert the rotary motion of the drive motor into linear motion of the axis. Just as before, each system works but each is a compromise.

We will start with two methods that work but are seldom used today. The first is to move the axis with a belt or chain. The drive motor turns a pulley or sprocket that the belt or chain is wrapped around. The ends of the belt are attached to the movable part of the axis.

This system can generate extremely fast movement but it is difficult to achieve the rigid level of positioning needed for router work. Nonetheless, I have seen some very low cost machines use this system and there is no reason that it can't perform well in less demanding applications.

The next system is one I have not seen in the U.S. but is used on machine tools in Russia. It is called a friction drive and consists of a polished steel bar on which a steel wheel rides. The drive wheel is pressed into the bar with a substantial force and friction between the bar and the wheel is used to move the axis. The drive provides backlash free operation but has some other disadvantages.

Because the drive relies on friction and not a mechanical link like a gear, it can drift over time. To prevent this, they use a linear feedback system along the axis to determine position rather than the encoder on the servomotor. The CNC control must then resolve any conflict in position data from the two sources, that is the linear scale and the encoder on the servomotor. In Russia they used lasers as the linear feedback but they were limited to feed speeds that were too slow for woodworking. The system could work with glass scales, however this type of linear feedback is quite expensive and is difficult to cost justify today.

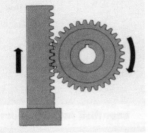

Rack and Pinion Drive

The two most common drives today are the rack and the ball screw. The rack consists of a long steel bar into which gear teeth have been cut. The drive motor turns a pinion gear that is meshed into this rack. As the gear turns, it rolls up and down the rack moving the axis. Although this system is rather simple it has some limitations.

The servomotor must turn at a reasonably high speed to generate the required power. It must therefore drive the pinion gear through a gear reduction box. For a gear of any kind to operate, there must be some clearance between the teeth. When gears are properly meshed together, they do not slide on each other. They roll on each other kind of like a rocking chair rolls on the floor. There must be some clearance between the backside of the gear tooth and the next gear to prevent these from sliding or scraping on each other. This clearance is called backlash. Some level of backlash must be present for pinion gears to operate. The gearbox may also have some backlash depending on the design.

Backlash can create some difficulty when operating a CNC router. The basic effect of backlash occurs when an axis reverses direction. The drive is moving the axis in one direction. When it stops, the gears are all solid in the direction that the axis was driving. When the drive reverses, it must first take up the backlash of the system before it begins to move the axis. For example, let us assume that the backlash was ten thousandths of an inch. When the axis reverses, it must move ten thousandths of an inch before the axis begins to move at all. Once the motion is complete, the axis will be ten thousandths of an inch short of the desired position because of the backlash.

The simplest way to adjust for this problem is by using backlash compensation in the CNC control. All this does is add the amount of backlash any time a drive changes direction. In the simple example, the reverse motion would be the distance programmed plus ten thousandths. In actual practice, the amount of backlash compensation actually put in the control is slightly less than the actual backlash but it reduces the error to such a small number that it doesn't matter.

Excessive backlash can create other problems that can't be corrected by backlash compensation. If the machine is operated to cause a lead error, the backlash may create a positional error even with compensation. This is especially true if the next motion is on the second axis.

Also, should the cutting forces become very large with a low friction machine, it can cause the axis to vibrate within the backlash creating a poor quality cut.

Although most machine manufacturers use one technique or another to try and eliminate backlash, if it can be reduced to five thousandths or less it is unlikely that it will have a noticeable effect on either performance or accuracy.

There are some methods for mechanically eliminating backlash in a rack system. One technique uses a split pinion gear. The gear is split into two gears and then the gears are spring loaded so that the teeth rotate apart. One gear contacts the front teeth of the rack and the other contacts the back teeth. Although this does eliminate backlash it does so by sliding one of the gears on the teeth resulting in substantially higher wear.

Another method uses two pinion gears, each driven by a different servomotor. One servomotor is controlled normally and the second is controlled to maintain a certain amount of force against the first motor. Again the teeth of one motor will be sliding instead of rolling and in this case a second drive system is required on each axis.

Rack drive systems have some other shortcomings. The gearbox required to drive the pinion gear is generally not more than 75% efficient and in many cases less. This means that a significant amount of the available power is used to overcome friction in the system. If you loosen the gears to decrease friction you introduce additional backlash. If you tighten the system to eliminate backlash you increase friction and decrease performance.

Because of these problems, the most common drive means for CNC routers is the ball screw. We have already discussed the ball screw design when we covered lead screw compensation. The lead screw compensation discussion also applies to screw drives.

A ball screw is about 98% efficient so it does not have the friction problem that the gear reduction drive has with a rack drive system. A ball screw will generally have some level of backlash, although it is possible to minimize it by selectively using different sized balls that exactly match the screw being used. Backlash can also be eliminated on a ball screw by using a second ball nut spring loaded against the first one. Unlike the spring-loaded system on the rack, this system does not cause sliding. The balls on both ball nuts roll properly so this arrangement does not significantly increase wear.

A Ball Screw System

Although lead screws seem to have the edge as a drive means today, they do have one major technical problem that must be addressed. This problem is commonly referred to as lead screw whip. If you take a long metal rod and begin to rotate it faster and faster, at some point you reach a rotation speed called critical speed. Any rotation speed above critical speed will cause the rod to wobble or whip back and forth. Operation below that speed will be steady and operation above that speed will be increasingly unstable.

Lead screws are, in fact, long metal rods and so they are affected by this tendency to whip above certain speeds.

Several factors affect critical speed. The rigidity or stiffness of the material affects critical speed. The stiffer the material that the screw is made of, the higher the critical speed. In the case of lead screws, however, they are all made of essentially hardened steel and so finding a material that is significantly stiffer is difficult.

The mounting method, that is the method by which the ends of the lead screw are mounted, also affects critical speed. Without getting into a great deal of engineering detail, the more rigid the end mounting, the higher the critical speed. This is an area where machine manufacturers can improve the situation although rigid multi-bearing mounting assemblies are more expensive.

If you examine a typical lead screw on a CNC router you will find that the lead, that is the amount that the screw advances the axis per revolution is typically one inch. With a one-inch lead and feed speeds normally found on CNC routers today, the lead screw is well into critical speed.

One method of addressing the whip problem is to increase the lead of the screw. In this case, each revolution of the screw moves the axis two or three inches instead of one inch. Thus, the required feed speeds can be obtained with lower rotation speed of the lead screw. These types of screws are typically called high helix screws.

There are some shortcomings with these screws, however. Since they rotate slower, some means of gear or belt reduction is needed to allow the servomotor to operate at the higher rotational speeds where it is efficient and yet drive the lead screw at a slower speed. This reduction can be a source of design problems and perhaps backlash if it is not engineered properly.

Because of their geometry, high helix screws are generally not constructed using the same methods as the more typical half inch or one inch lead screws. This different construction method tends to make high helix screws more expensive. It also tends to give them less overall thrust capacity. Again, the thrust capacity of most lead screws today is many times greater than that required to operate the machine so don't let a fast talking machine salesman scare you about lead screw capacity. If the machine performs well in production and exhibits a good long operating life the lead screw choice made by the machine manufacturer was a good one. When we discuss some of these design factors we are simply trying to show you why some manufacturers design their machines one way and others select a different set of design parameters.

Maintaining accuracy with a high helix screw is more difficult. A rotational error on a high helix screw will have two or three times the impact of that same rotational error on a standard lead screw.

Despite their higher cost, high helix screws are successfully used in a variety of applications and are relatively common on point to point machines where very high feed speeds are common. Again, there is an engineering compromise that must be made between screw cost, accuracy, motor rotation speed, power and screw whip.

Another way to address screw whip is to not rotate the screw. By rigidly fixing the ends of the screw and rotating the ball nut instead, critical speed can be increased. There still is a critical speed but it tends to be higher than when the screw is rotated. If you don't rotate the screw, why should there be a critical speed at all?

In practice, the interaction of the ball nut and screw at certain speeds will induce screw whip even if the screw is not turning. The factors that influence screw whip are closely associated with the natural harmonic frequency of the screw. This is the frequency at which the screw will vibrate if hit. This is somewhat like a guitar string vibrates when it is plucked. When screw operation inputs forces at or near this natural frequency, the screw can begin to vibrate, Each cycle the vibration gets greater until the screw is whipping. This is something like a person walking over a long footbridge. Sometimes the frequency of the steps matches the frequency of the bridge and the bridge begins to bounce. Each step makes the bounce higher. This same phenomenon occurs with a fixed lead screw and a ball nut.

The most common way to address lead screw whip is to use a larger diameter lead screw. For a specific length, the larger the diameter of the lead screw the higher the critical speed. To prevent screw whip completely, simply make the lead screw diameter large enough so that the critical speed is higher than any possible operating speed. This does work and it works well for eliminating lead screw whip but, as always, there is another price to pay. The obvious price is a more expensive lead screw but it goes beyond this.

When we discussed drive motors we focused carefully on obtaining the best acceleration and deceleration possible. We also noted that the mass of the rotor of the drive motor was a major factor in performance. After the inertia of the motor rotor, the rotary inertia of the lead screw is the next most important factor in overall system performance. The larger in diameter the lead screw, the more difficult it is to get it rotating and to stop it from rotating. The inertia increases as the square of the diameter. If a lead screw is twice as large, it does not have twice the inertia, it has four times the inertia. It is four times harder to get moving and four times harder to stop than the smaller lead screw.

We can resort to a larger servomotor to power the larger screw but that costs more and requires a larger rotor that reduces performance from the motor. A larger lead screw, while it does reduce or eliminate whip generally provides somewhat lower overall performance than the smaller diameter lead screw.

Thermwood Anti-whip System

Thermwood has developed and patented a system that allows a smaller, lower inertial lead screw to operate above critical speed without screw whip. The device is simply a nylon guide with a C shaped cutout. The lead screw fits into the cutout. The device is positioned to support the lead screw somewhere near the middle. The lead screw turns inside the guide. The guide prevents the lead screw from moving back and forth in any plane and thus prevents it from setting up whip. It is a little like placing a bearing in the center of the lead screw to support it. The lead screw then operates as two shorter lead screws that each has a much higher critical speed.

When the axis needs to move from one side of the guide to the other it simply pushes the guide out of the way as it goes by. Once the axis mechanism is clear of the guide, the guide moves back into position to again support the lead screw. While the axis is passing the guide, the ball nut acts as the support guide so the anti-whip guide isn't needed.

This system works well, is relatively inexpensive and allows a smaller diameter high-performance screw to operate well above critical speed without encountering problems with screw whip.

Again, with the drive means, each of the systems discussed can be made to work and work well. It is more important that you determine that the machine designers who developed the machine you are considering properly understand the underlying technology. If they do, they will properly address the shortcomings and limitations of the method they have chosen and the system will perform well. Again it is important to look at actual system performance rather than try and determine theoretically which is the better system.

The next item we will discuss is the linear slides or rails. Again there are several methods that all work reasonably well and again, each has advantages and shortcomings. One or two of these systems are used extensively however, each has been used on CNC routers in the past and some may show up again in the future.

Dovetail Slide

There are some systems used in the metalworking industry that are not normally found in woodworking. The simple dovetail slide is one of those systems. The slide is made up of a ground and polished metal slide, flat on top with edges that turn back like a dovetail. The carrier is machined to fit this dovetail, generally with an adjustable bar along one edge. This carrier simply slides along the polished slide relying on some type of lubrication to reduce sliding friction. This system offers a highly rigid slide with very high load carrying capacity. Some of the shortcomings of this system, however, are reducing its use, even in metalworking machines.

The system exhibits a high level of friction, especially when loaded. With proper lubrication this is not a problem, especially at lower speeds. As feed speeds increase, the friction, besides reducing system performance, also generates heat. This heat can become excessive in high feed speed applications and bind the carrier and slide in extreme instances.

The need for a constant level of lubrication makes it difficult to operate in a wood environment. Sawdust that collects on the slide can absorb the lubricant and carry it away as the sawdust is pushed off the slide during operation.

The final shortcoming for wood applications is a life that is too short at the feed speeds common in woodworking operations. The high friction tends to wear the slide. The slide can be adjusted for this wear to some extent, however, it is common for the wear to be greater near the center of the slide where the carrier moves most of the time and less at the ends. If you adjust the slide to be tight in the center it won't move to the ends because it jams. If you adjust it properly at the ends, the center is too loose. At this point, the slide must be rebuilt or replaced.

A variation of the system is used in large metalworking machine and is used on some axes in the woodworking industry. This system substitutes a polymer material on the slide carrier for the metal gibes. In addition to the other advantages, that is a rigid structure and high weight capacity, this system offers much lower friction and lower wear than the metal slide.

There are two types of polymer used for this purpose, thermoset and thermoplastic. A thermoset is a liquid plastic that undergoes a chemical reaction when processed and turns into a solid. Some common thermosets are polyester in fiberglass and epoxy commonly used in two part adhesives. Once a thermoset has reacted it will not turn back to a liquid again.

Thermoplastics are plastic materials that soften when heated above a certain point and harden again when cooled below that point. Each time a thermoplastic is heated it will soften.

Because of their lower friction levels, polymer slides can handle higher average feed speeds than metal slides. They have been successfully used on vertical axes of woodworking machines where the high rigidity is important but, we are not aware of this material being used on any of the long major axes.

Some of these materials are impregnated with lubricants and can operate without external lubrication. Some of these materials were developed for the space program for use in space where liquid lubricants freeze. This feature can eliminate some of the problems associated with liquid lubricants in a wood environment.

Application of a polymer slide material is actually quite complex. There are two types of friction, static and dynamic. Static friction is the friction that exists between two surfaces that are stopped and resting against each other. It is the friction that resists sliding one object against the other from a stop. Dynamic friction is the friction between two surfaces as they move against each other. It is the constant resistance as you slide one surface against another.

Static friction is generally greater than dynamic friction. You must push harder on an object to beak it loose and get it moving. Once moving it requires less force to keep it moving. This characteristic is sometimes called stickshion.

Material that exhibits stickshion is difficult to control using a servo system and should be avoided. There are some materials, however, whose static friction and dynamic friction are almost identical. These materials are ideal for use on machine tool slides and in fact, they are used extensively for that purpose in metalworking.

Another approach that further eliminates friction is to use a steel bar and recirculating roller bearings. This system offers very high load capacity and good rigid construction, however, it only provides support in one direction. To develop the all around support needed, several roller bearings are required sometimes opposing each other. Although this system works well it tends to be more expensive than required and is only used today on heavier machines where the load capacity is needed to carry the weight of the moving components.

Round Way and Round Way Linear Bearing

On the other end of the scale is the round way and linear bearing. The round way is a ground, polished rod on which rides a recirculating ball bearing. Round ways come in a variety of diameters and load capacities. It offers two major advantages. It is low cost and it has very low friction.

Because the round way and linear bearing is actually a round ball riding on a round shaft, the contact between the ball and the shaft is a single point. Even though there are a number of balls to carry the load, the load carrying capacity of this system tends to be lower than the other systems we have discussed.

The ball nut wraps about three-quarters of the way around the shaft being open at the bottom to allow clearance for the way support. This construction method means that the load carrying capacity of the system is different depending on the direction of the applied forces. Pushing toward the support rail offers full load capacity. Forces perpendicular to the support rail have a reduced capacity, typically 70% of rated load. Forces pulling away from the support rail may see the load capacity cut almost in half.

This characteristic must be taken into account when the fundamental design of the machine is first developed. It means that either the designer must configure the axes so that forces are applied in the optimum direction or must specify larger round ways that can handle the loads in a less than optimum configuration.

Track way and Track way Linear Bearing

Today, the most popular slide system is the track way. A track way is essentially a steel bar into which has been machined four concave tracks. A recirculating set of ball bearings rides in each of these tracks.

The track way has several advantages over the round way. Because you have a convex ball riding in a concave track, contact between the ball and the track is a line rather than a point. This means that the load capacity of each ball is greater and therefore, the load carrying capacity of a track way is several times greater than the load capacity of an equal sized round way. Also, because of the opposing orientation of the four tracks, the load capacity of the track way bearing is essentially the same regardless of the direction that the force is applied. This tends to make the track way more rigid overall than a similar sized round way.

The only real disadvantage of the track way is that it tends to cost more than a similar sized round way.

Again, the machine designer is faced with a series of selections for the machine ways. Applied properly, each will perform well. If you ignore the limitations, however, problems can occur. Again, the best way to determine if the design is adequate is to see how systems in the field are performing and how well they hold up over time.

The next area we are going to discuss is the router spindle. The technology in this area is quite complex and there is a lot of misinformation about spindles in the industry. Essentially there are two different types of spindles in use, the belt driven stand-alone spindle and the motor spindle.

The earliest spindles used for routing were the belt driven spindles. They consisted of a spindle housing with bearings at both ends that supported the spindle shaft. On one end of the spindle shaft was a collet or other arrangement to hold the router bit and on the other end was a pulley through which the spindle was driven. To obtain high router speeds the electric drive motor was equipped with a large diameter pulley and the spindle shaft was equipped with a small diameter pulley. If the motor pulley was four times larger in diameter than the spindle pulley, the spindle would rotate four times faster than the motor.

The routing process can consume several horsepower and so the drive belt must be capable of transmitting the necessary horsepower. The early spindles used wide flat belts running on flat pulleys. These were capable of transmitting the required horsepower between the drive motors and the spindle.

This type of spindle was primarily used on fixed routers, such as pin routers. The flat belt driven spindle was used successfully on early CNC routers although the package was large and somewhat heavy. Today the flat belt driven spindle is not used on CNC routers although Thermwood has developed a variation that is used extensively.

In the fundamental design, the Thermwood spindle has two basic changes from the original flat belt driven spindle. First, it does not use a flat belt, but instead, it uses a modern design poly-V belt. This belt uses a set of formed ridges along the belt to increase surface area and drive capability. This means that a belt that is less than an inch wide can transmit ten horsepower where it would require a five or six inch wide flat belt to transmit the same power. The second fundamental change to the design is that the driven pulley is located at the bottom of the spindle shaft, just above the collet instead of on the opposite end of the spindle. Thermwood engineers believe that you obtain a better drive with less spindle stress by driving the spindle as close to the cutting area as possible. Although substantially smaller than the original flat belt driven spindles, the Thermwood spindle is still much larger than the same horsepower motor spindle.

One potential problem with driving the spindle near the cutting area is that the pulleys and belts are subject to sawdust. Without effective protection, sawdust will build up on the pulleys, increase the tension on the belt and possibly destroy the balance of the motor or the spindle.

To prevent this from occurring, Thermwood runs both the drive pulley and the spindle pulley inside a closed chamber. The chamber is pressurized with compressed air to provide a small positive pressure inside the chamber. Any possible hole through which sawdust could enter has air leaking out of it. This effectively prevents anything from entering, even in highly contaminated environments.

As CNC routers became more popular, demand developed for a router spindle that was smaller and lighter than the belt driven spindles of the day. It was determined that a synchronous motor wound to rotate at 3,600 RPM on 60 cycle electric current would turn at 18,000 RPM if operated on 300 cycle current. To obtain the 300 Hz frequency, engineers took a standard 60Hz electric motor operating at 3600 RPM and coupled it directly to a generator that produced 300Hz current when turned at 3,600 RPM. The result was current that would drive the motor at 18,000 RPM.

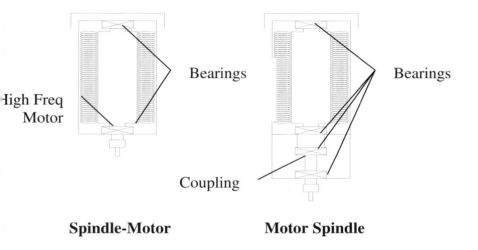

Spindle-Motor   **Motor Spindle**

To turn this motor into a router spindle they simply added a collet arrangement at one end to hold the router bit. Although it worked, problems quickly developed. The typical spindle motor had a single ball bearing at each end designed to handle the rotational forces of the motor. These bearings now needed to handle not only the motor loads but also the cutting forces generated by the routing process. Also, heat generated by the routing process was introduced directly to the motor shaft exposing the bearings to the heat. With higher loads, faster speeds and higher heat, bearing life was reduced drastically.

To address this situation, a separate spindle with its own bearings was coupled in-line with the motor. This arrangement became known as a motor-spindle. In this arrangement the motor had two bearings and the spindle had two bearings. The spindle bearings could now handle the cutting forces while the motor bearings were again only required to handle the motor loads. This arrangement worked better in most applications but some other problems developed.

The bearings used for the spindle are an angular contact ball bearing. This means that the balls of the bearing contact the bearing race at an angle. A router bit is subject to two forces. The first is the radial load. As you push the bit through the work a opposing force pushing against the bit is developed. The primary purpose of the bearing is to resist this force.

As you push on the bottom of the tool, straight into the spindle you develop the second force, axial force. This is the type of load developed when you plunge the router bit into the workpiece. Also, certain tools, especially shaper cutters create both radial loads and axial loads.

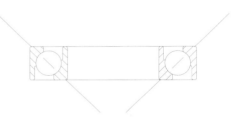

Angular Contact Ball Bearing

The contact angle of the angular contact ball bearing determines the ratio of radial force to axial force that the bearing can withstand. A zero angle bearing will have all the bearing capacity in the radial direction but will have little axial capacity. As the angle increases, the axial capacity increases but the radial capacity decreases. Determining the correct bearing angle for a spindle is a difficult decision. In most applications the designers have specified 90% or so of the bearing capacity for radial loads assuming that typical applications are primarily radial. When an application occurs where more axial loads are generated, the bearings fail early.

One common cause of bearing failure from excessive axial loads is trying to plunge into the workpiece with a router bit that is not designed as a plunge bit. Some tools are intended to plunge directly into the work, however, most are not. Using a non-plunge bit to plunge into the work will generate substantial axial loads and will quickly fail bearings designed primarily for radial loads.

One answer for this is to add a bearing at the bottom of the spindle that is primarily intended to handle the axial loads along with the standard bearing intended to handle radial loads. This two bearing set can resist both axial and radial loads.

Companies that build both the spindle and the machine can coordinate the design of the spindle to the drive forces of the machine. This means that the axial capacity of the spindle can be made greater than the ability of the machine to push down. In this case, the machine is incapable of destroying the bearings through excessive axial loads.

A second problem that has occurred with the motor-spindle is in the area of the coupling between the motor and the spindle. In this area we are trying to transmit high horsepower at very high speed. If we rigidly couple these two, we will set up vibration and forces that will quickly destroy the adjoining bearings. Any misalignment between the motor and spindle will also put stress on the bearings, quickly destroying them. Therefore, some type of flexible coupling is required. Most standard flexible couplings can't operate at normal routing speeds.

The method that major manufacturers settled on is to cut a keyway in the top of the spindle shaft and a matching keyway in the bottom of the motor shaft. A metal key is then inserted in the keyways connecting the shafts. When the shafts are aligned both axially and angular, this arrangement seems to work well. Any misalignment, however, results in the metal key sliding against the shaft 18,000 times a minute. This creates heat that is transmitted up and down the two shafts and ultimately to the bearings.

Instead of resorting to a separate spindle, some manufacturers simply installed a double bearing set on the bottom of a spindle motor. This generally requires larger diameter bearings to fit over the taper of the collet, which restricts the maximum bit shank diameter that the spindle can accommodate. Except for this limitation, the system seems to work reasonably well.

Another factor that seems to have a major impact on bearing life is the fit of the bearing into the bearing seat. The bearing seat is machined into the spindle housing. This seat is generally slightly smaller than the outer diameter of the bearing. The bearing is then pressed into this seat. The press fit actually shrinks the outer race of the bearing slightly so prior to pressing into place, the bearing must be made slightly larger than needed. This fit is extremely important and is quite difficult to machine accurately.

The axial alignment of the bearing seats is also extremely important. If the bearings are slightly out of alignment they will be under a load even before any external cuttings loads are applied. A slight error in seat diameter and a slight error in alignment can easily place the bearings under enough load to use up half or more of the total bearing capacity. A bearing in this condition will fail early compared to a bearing properly installed.

Thermwood has developed and patented a simple system to assure proper bearing alignment on its belt driven spindles. They use a bearing that has the proper fit between the inner and outer race without compression from pressing it into a seat. The bearing seats are machined substantially oversized and then the bearings are chemically bonded into place using a special polymeric material. Since the polymer is a liquid that sets into a solid, it can exert no force on the bearing during the assembly process. The result is a perfectly aligned bearing with no assembly stresses.

Most router spindles use standard bearings with ground and polished balls. The steel ball offers a hard, rigid surface that is also somewhat elastic. The hard surface provides a long operating life at high speed and the resilient nature of steel offers a bearing that can handle shock loads and slight levels of contamination.

These standard bearings seem to work well for high-speed applications until the speed reaches about 30,000 RPM. As the bearing speed increases beyond this point, the centrifugal force of the steel balls spinning around the race start to become significant. As the bearing spins the balls are trying to fly out of the bearing but are held in place by the outer race. The rather heavy weight of the balls can create forces at high speeds that approach the capacity of the bearing. This leaves very little capacity left for handling the actual cutting loads.

For very high speed applications, typically 30,000 to 80,000 RPM, a different type of bearing is used. In this new bearing the inner and outer bearing races are still made of steel but the balls are made of a ceramic material. These ceramic balls have a very hard outer surface yet they are very light weight. Their light weight means that at high speeds they do not develop near the internal forces of a steel ball. The amount of force developed is directly proportional to the weight of the balls.

Using ceramic balls, we can again offer a reasonable load capacity at very high-speed operation. There is, however some downside to using ceramic bearings. Unlike the steel balls, ceramic balls are not as resilient. They are somewhat brittle and can shatter under a shock load. They are less tolerant of slight contamination and are generally not as rugged.

In general, for speeds up to about 30,000 RPM, standard steel balls provide the best combination of capacity, life and resilience. For speeds above 30,000 RPM ceramic bearings will be required but the resulting bearing will be less tolerant of misuse.

Bearing lubrication is an important part of spindle life. There are two generally accepted methods of lubricating high-speed bearings, grease and oil. The grease used for high speed spindle bearings is a special material. Normal lubricating grease will burn out spindle bearings in well under an hour. Grease bearings are available in two forms. One bearing is sealed and greased for life. The other type is designed to be re-lubricated at regular intervals.

In general the type of bearing that is re-lubricated will offer a better life than permanently lubricated bearings, provided the lubrication process is done properly. Over many years we have determined that this is almost never done properly in a furniture factory. There are many errors that can be made and any of these errors will result in premature bearing failure.

The most common error is over lubricating. The bearings are designed to operate with very little grease. If too much grease is introduced into the bearing, it will quickly heat up and fail. If the grease zert is not properly cleaned, dirt on the zert will be introduced into the bearing and it will fail quickly. Incorrect grease will cause early failure.

Although the re-lubricated bearing has the potential for the better life, in actual practice the permanently lubricated bearing exhibits better real life in a furniture factory environment.

The second basic lubrication material is oil. The oil is generally introduced into the bearing as an air-oil mist. This mist is a fine spray of compressed air into which has been suspended fine particles of oil. This type of lubrication offers several advantages. First, since a fine stream of air is being introduced into the bearing, the air escaping every opening in the bearing effectively blocks contamination from entering the bearing. The fine oil mist provides a minimum level of lubrication but does not build up and cause heat. The air and oil moving through the bearing actually provides forced cooling that results in better bearing life.

Overall, air-oil lubrication offers the best lubrication method but there is a price to pay. The systems required to create the mist and then transfer it to the bearings is expensive and requires ongoing maintenance. A failure of these systems will result in a bearing failure in short order. The air used to power the lubrication system must be dry and free of contamination or, again bearing failure will result. You must also make certain that the exhausting air mist does not condense oil on any part of the machine or spindle where it can drip on the workpiece and ruin it. Some spindles actually try and condense the oil and offer systems to collect and dispose of this material.

As with all other aspects of CNC router design, either lubrication system can work well if properly designed. Again proper design can only be judged by looking at operating results in typical production environments.

When high frequency spindles were first introduced, they were powered by a motor-generator set as we described earlier. The electric output of a motor-generator is a perfect sine wave. The spindle motor is designed to operate with a perfect sine wave. Eventually, electronic frequency converters began to replace the more expensive motor-generators for powering high-frequency spindle motors. With the electronic frequency converters came some new problems.

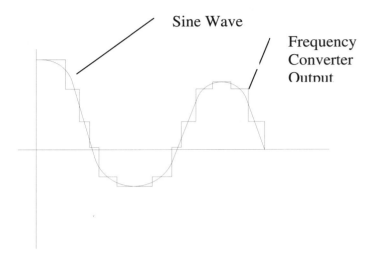

Sine Wave

Frequency
Converter
Output

Sine Wave versus Square Wave Frequency Converter Output

An electronic frequency converter is basically a digital device so producing a smooth sine wave is quite difficult. The electric output of an electronic frequency converter is therefore a modified square wave. This wave shape approximates a sine wave, however, there are areas where the wave form varies from a true sine wave. Wherever the modified square wave is outside the sine wave, the extra power can't be used by the motor and produces heat instead of torque. When the modified square wave is inside the sine wave, lower torque is produced resulting in a loss of power. The final result is that the spindle motor runs hotter than normal and produces less power than normal.

When manufacturers first began using high frequency spindle motors they discovered that these motors did not seem to have as much power as standard synchronous motor driven spindles. A five horsepower synchronous motor powered spindle seemed to have much more power than a five horsepower high-frequency spindle. How can this be if both motors are the same horsepower?

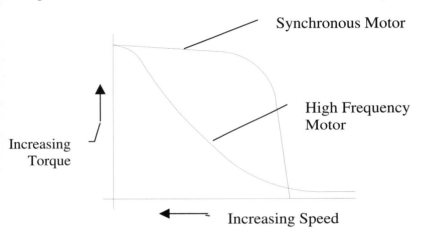

Synchronous Motor

High Frequency
Motor

Increasing
Torque

Increasing Speed

Torque versus Speed Curves

Horsepower is essentially torque times speed. It is determined by using the rotating torque available at full speed. In most cases this is a purely theoretical number determined using the amount of power the motor draws. As you load the motor by cutting, for example, the speed is reduced. The amount of torque available from the motor at these reduced speeds also changes. A graph of the available torque at various operating speeds is called the torque-speed curve.

The torque-speed graph of a synchronous motor shows that as speed is reduced, torque remains relatively constant until a certain point where the torque drops off rather quickly. On a high-frequency motor, however, torque drops off as speed is reduced. Since horsepower is speed times torque, a synchronous motor's horsepower drops off as it begins to cut because the rotation speed is lower. The horsepower of a high-frequency motor, however, drops off much faster since both components of horsepower are lower. Not only is the rotation speed lower but the torque is also lower.

Thus, both motors have the same horsepower rating but when actually cutting there is less horsepower available from a typical high-frequency motor than from a synchronous motor. Thus, it is common to see ten or fifteen horsepower in a high frequency spindle when a five horsepower manual router operated by a synchronous motor has more than enough power for most applications.

How much actual power is required for CNC routing? In actual measurements of current draw we found that the actual power consumed by a properly operating system is much less than expected. Most applications required between one and two horsepower with the most demanding applications seldom using more than three horsepower. From a practical standpoint this means that most router spindles offered on machines today are capable of handling the demands of normal CNC routing. Spindle life, on the other hand, should be determined from actual field experience by current machine users. It is virtually impossible to determine from design parameters alone whether or not a particular spindle design will provide an acceptable life.

In order to machine a wood part on a CNC router the part must be held securely in place. This seems obvious, however, this is the one area that most new CNC router users underestimate. The hold down system has a significant impact on part accuracy, quality of finish and at times even feed speeds and tooling life. There are two things that should be understood about part hold down: holding the part securely is important and there is no one system that will properly hold all parts.

There are a wide variety of hold-down systems available today. Each works well for a certain type of part. We will examine each of these systems and explain which system works best with each type of part.

The purpose of the hold-down system is to hold the part in place for machining. This is so basic that people underestimate what holding the part in place means. A vacuum hold-down where the part rests on rubber seals may allow the part to move or wiggle slightly on the soft seals. This can easily result in excessive tooling marks, chatter and a poor quality edge. When this occurs, people tend to blame the machine, the cutters or the material where the hold down system is the real culprit. It is also possible that under the pressure of cutting the part may move slightly resulting in a loss of accuracy.

Holding the part rigidly in place is important. It is much more important if you are trying to achieve a smooth machined edge and less important if you are simply looking for a specific shape for a non-cosmetic part.

Generally the table is covered with a sheet of plywood, particleboard or other material on to which the parts are clamped or the fixtures clamped. This table covering is referred to as a spoilboard or a wasteboard depending on the machine manufacturer you are talking to. We will call it a spoilboard in the book.

The major purpose of the spoilboard is to protect the table when you are cutting all the way through a part. Many times the hold down method is incorporated directly into the spoilboard. Other times a fixture for the part is mounted to the spoilboard. There are other times where the spoilboard is an integral part of the hold-down system.

The most basic hold-down system is to simply nail or bolt the part down. Some parts have interior holes or are not cosmetic at all and it is possible to simply attach the part to the spoilboard mechanically. Except for machining very small parts, this is seldom used for production but is common for one-up parts or prototypes where the operator doesn't want to stop and build a fixture for one part. Obviously, the time required to fasten the part down and then remove it make this system impractical for most production operations, not to mention the hole it leaves in the part. There are exceptions to this however. I have seen small Derringer pistol handles held down through a counterbored hole in the center. These were very small parts that could be completely machined using this hold-down method.

Side Activated Hand Clamp

Hand operated clamps offer a practical method of mechanically holding the part in place for a much wider variety of parts. Properly applied these offer a highly rigid support for the part. There is a wide variety of mechanical clamps available however they tend to fall into two basic types, those that clamp the part to the table top and those that push the part into a fence or guide.

Top Acting Hand Clamp

Generally if you are going to work on the edge of the part you will need to clamp the face of the part to the table top leaving the edge exposed. If you are going to work on the face of the part you will need to clamp the edge of the part into a guide or fence. In this arrangement the guide or fence should be designed to pull the part down to the table top as well as clamp the edge.

Fence Locating Fixture

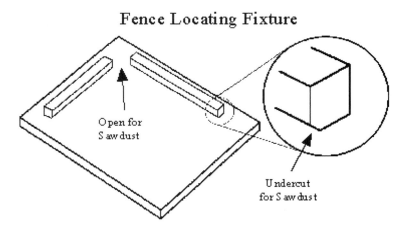

Open for
Sawdust

Undercut
for Sawdust

If you are using a guide fence, it is a good idea to leave the corner open to prevent sawdust from collecting and affecting the positioning of the part. In the same manner it is a good idea to relieve the bottom edge of the fence where it meets the tabletop to minimize the effect of the small amount of sawdust that will collect in these areas.

Mechanical clamps offer a good alternative if you are going to work on one, or perhaps two edges of a part. If, however, you need to machine all four edges, clamps don't work well since on at least one edge the clamp itself will be in the way.

Air, or pneumatic powered clamps have been used in these circumstances. By placing one clamp along one edge of the part and a second clamp along a second edge, all four edges can be machined. As the cutter approaches the first clamp, it retracts under machine control while the second clamp holds the part in place. Once the edge has been completed, the first clamp again clamps the part down.

The process is repeated with the second clamp. As the head approaches the clamp retracts while the first clamp holds the part. This does work, but there are simpler methods of holding a part that must be machined on all four edges.

The advantages of mechanical clamps are that they are inexpensive, easy to understand and offer a highly rigid mounting when properly applied. They may be the only practical hold-down method for small or odd-shaped parts that do not have enough surface area for some of the vacuum hold-down systems.

The most common system for holding parts on a CNC router is conventional vacuum. Vacuum does not actually hold the part. Vacuum is simply the absence of air. The approximately 20 mile thick layer of air surrounding the Earth has weight. At the surface of the Earth it weighs about 14 pounds per square inch. The air, being a fluid, pushes on everything in all directions equally so no force is exerted on objects.

When the air is removed from one side of an object, the air on the other side now pushes against the object. This is the basis of vacuum hold-down. The part to be machined is sealed against the tabletop or a fixture and then the air inside the seal is removed using a vacuum pump. The air on the outside then pushes the part against the fixture.

Essentially with conventional vacuum all you are doing is weighing down the part using the air pressure of the atmosphere. How much weight does the air pressure actually put on the part?

As we said earlier, the air weighs about 14 pounds per square inch. This level actually varies each day and can be determined by noting the barometric pressure in the weather report. Conventional vacuum actually works slightly better some days than others. Thus if you could achieve a perfect vacuum you could achieve about 14 pounds of force per square inch. It is virtually impossible to achieve this level of vacuum however. In practice with a well-sealed system, a good pump and material that does not leak you can consistently achieve about 10 pounds of force per square inch.

Thus a one foot by one foot part has 144 square inches of area if the seal is located at the very edge of the part. At ten pounds per square inch this part would be held in place with 1,440 pounds of force. As you can see, this is a considerable force. It is like piling over 1,400 pounds of weight on the part and yet the part is left completely accessible for machining, free of weight or clamps.

Obviously as the area inside the seal gets smaller the amount of holding force gets less. A six-inch by six-inch part has 36 square inches inside the seal and so is held in place by 360 pounds. Heavy cuts in hard material may produce enough side force to move this part. A three-inch by three-inch part has nine square inches or ninety pounds of holding force. The hold down method is now getting quite marginal. There are a few techniques that help to hold smaller parts.

A common method to assist vacuum hold-down where the back surface of the part is not critical is to install barbs or metal points in the fixture so they stab the back of the part when it is loaded. The air pressure pushes the part against the barbs making it more difficult to slide. Forces during cutting are generally side forces trying to slide the part. The barbs can help prevent this.

If the back surface is more critical, adhesive backed sandpaper can be installed on the fixture inside the seal. Again the air pressure presses the part against the sandpaper, increasing friction and making it more difficult to slide the part.

Eventually part size gets too small and it is necessary to resort to another hold-down method. There are also other factors that reduce the effectiveness of conventional vacuum and must be considered.

As we have seen, to make conventional vacuum work we must remove the air on one side of the part. This may be much more difficult than it sounds. Air, being a thin fluid is trying desperately to get back into the evacuated area. This is one reason for the seal. Air leakage through the seal area can reduce the effectiveness of vacuum hold-down to the point where it no longer functions effectively. The seal material must be soft and pliable enough to prevent air leakage and yet strong enough to withstand repeated loading and unloading of parts without becoming damaged.

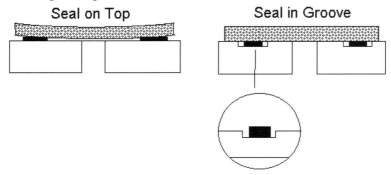

The seal material should be placed in a machined groove cut into the fixture rather than directly on top of the fixture. No more than one third to one half of the seal height should extend above the top surface of the fixture. When the part is pulled down the seal will then collapse to perhaps one half of its normal height. If the seal is placed on top of the fixture, directly between the fixture and the part, when the part is pulled down, thousands of pounds of force will be pressing on the seal trying to smash it completely flat. This will quickly break down almost any seal material. It will also cause the part to warp with the center pulled down to the face of the fixture but the edges raised up on the seal. Neither of these is a good thing.

The seal area, however, is not the only source for air leaks. The part itself can be a problem. Many wood and composite wood materials are somewhat porous. Air can actually leak through the part. At this point the flow capacity of the vacuum pump determines whether or not the system will work. Some level of vacuum can be established. Whether or not this level will be adequate depends on many factors including part size, pump capacity and amount of leakage. At times, people have laid brown paper or newspaper on top of the part to help seal its front surface and reduce air leakage.

Air can also leak through the fixture. Many companies like to make vacuum fixtures from high quality plywood. The hole through the center of the fixture through which air is removed exposes the edge of the plywood to vacuum. It is common for air to leak between the layers of plywood rendering the fixture ineffective. In these cases it is necessary to seal the vacuum hole and the top surface of the fixture in order for it to work properly. The hole and plywood edges can be sealed with simple wood filler and the surface can be sealed with any good paint sealer.

Conventional vacuum offers a good, reliable, low cost and effective hold-down method for CNC routers. The only real disadvantage to conventional vacuum as we have described it so far is that you are required to build a vacuum fixture for each part you wish to process. Several methods have been developed to try and get around this requirement.

Pod systems use vacuum pods of approximately three-inch diameter. These pods are mounted on some type of adjustable slide mechanism. To fixture a part, pods are moved and secured under the part. Pods may be round, square or rectangular depending on the manufacturer. Pods work reasonably well for larger parts although setting up a pod system for several parts may actually take longer than loading a single vacuum fixture that has already been built to accommodate those parts. If parts are to be manufactured more than one time, building a fixture may be more economical. If parts are only going to be run once or twice, the pod system may be the better choice. You should also note that the amount of holding force with a pod system tends to be less than a custom made vacuum fixture. The pods are also connected mechanically to the machine so any movement at the attachment point may result in a less rigid hold-down.

Carter flop-pod System

A patented system called the Carter Flip-Pod System offers a novel approach. The Carter Pod consists of a molded plastic pod approximately three inches in diameter. This pod has a lip along one edge that fits into a recess machined into a vacuum plenum that covers the entire tabletop. The pod can be inserted into the plenum in two different orientations. In one orientation, the pod fits down into the plenum with its top surface flush with the tabletop. A small rubber ball inside the pod covers the vacuum access hole sealing it off. In this orientation the pod is inactive.

If the pod is flipped over, however, it extends a couple of inches above the tabletop exposing a vacuum seal. The ball inside the pod falls from the vacuum hole, opening it up and the pod is active. Setting up this system requires that the pods you wish to use be simply flipped over.

Again, the system works reasonably well and because the pod is machined into the tabletop, it offers a fairly rigid mounting. Just like the other pods, however, the amount of holding area is less than a full custom vacuum fixture.

Both a custom vacuum fixture and a pod system share the requirement that they be set-up each time the part to be machined changes. When the production batch size become very small, one or two parts, this can become a major disruption. A system that is more universal would be a major benefit.

Earlier we mentioned that air would actually leak through certain materials. This is especially true of certain types of particleboard and MDF. This fact can be used to develop a type of universal hold-down although it has some limitations.

Turbine Vacuum Pump

To make this system work, a different type of vacuum pump is needed. The conventional vacuum pump creates a fairly high level of vacuum but it does so with relatively small flows. A typical conventional vacuum pump has flow levels of 30 to 50 cubic feet per minute. To make this universal vacuum system work, flows of 500 to 1,000 cubic feet per minute are necessary. At these flow levels, the actual amount of vacuum will be substantially less than is normal with a conventional vacuum system.

Universal Vacuum Plenum

A particleboard tabletop is mounted to a vacuum plenum. The vacuum plenum is a sheet of plastic material about ¾ inch thick into which has been machined a pattern that looks much like a waffle iron. This exposes much of the underside of the particleboard to the vacuum chamber while still supporting the material. When the universal vacuum pump is connected to the plenum and turned on, air is constantly pulled through the particleboard. The flow capacity of the pump is actually greater than the total leakage across the entire tabletop. This maintains a vacuum under the tabletop and creates a very thin low-pressure area on top of the table. If a part is laid in this low-pressure area, the amount of air on the underside is less than the amount on top of the part and it is held in place. This works without the need for seals. It also works even if there are grooves cut in the particleboard top from previous parts.

The amount of holding force available from universal vacuum is substantially less than that available from conventional vacuum. Whereas conventional vacuum can develop up to ten pounds per square inch, universal vacuum generally works between two and four pounds per square inch. A two-foot by two-foot part is held in place by one to two thousand pounds of force, which is more than adequate for most applications. A one-foot by one-foot part is held in place by three to five hundred pounds of force, which is nearing the lower limit of hold-down requirements.

Although universal vacuum can hold a part without need for fixtures or set-up, its lower size limit is less than conventional vacuum. Also, the part must be relatively smooth and flat.

The low-pressure area developed on the tabletop by universal vacuum is only a few thousandths of an inch thick. For a part to be held in place it must move into this thin low-pressure area. Parts with a rough surface, such as plywood, cannot move close enough to the tabletop and thus will not be held in place properly. Also, a part that is warped will not move into the low-pressure area and thus will not be held down properly. In general universal vacuum works with smooth, flat parts that are at least a square foot in size. Once these requirements are met, the system works very well in practice.

Some manufacturers that do not offer universal vacuum have claimed in print that the particleboard top used in universal vacuum tends to fill with sawdust over time and quits working. In actual practice this does not seem to occur. The amount of force created by the vacuum and the airflow at any point on the surface are both quite low. Because of this there is not enough force to draw the sawdust that falls on the tabletop deep into the pores of the top. Simply blowing on the surface with compressed air seems to easily clean the surface and problems with plugging the particleboard top have simply not developed in practice.

If parts change often and are both large enough and flat, universal vacuum offers an extremely simple and easy hold-down system without the need for set-up or fixtures.

The final hold-down system we will discuss is also somewhat universal in nature. It was originally designed to hold down plywood boat bulkheads for the marine industry. These parts are machined from large sheets of plywood, are relatively large and change almost every cycle. The plywood used was almost always warped and so a method was needed that would press the parts down to the tabletop for machining.

To accomplish this a set of four rubber-coated rollers was placed across the width of the worktable. Two of these rollers were placed in front of the router spindle and two of the rollers were placed in back of the spindle. The router spindle could move back and forth between the rollers and when the spindle moved front to back the rollers moved with the spindle. The rollers actually pinched the part to the tabletop rolling over the top of the part as it moved front to back.

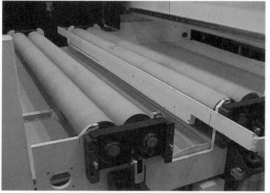

Roller Hold Down without Covers

Although the system works well, it also has some limitations. In order to hold a part properly, at least two rolls must contact the part. Because of clearance requirements this means that the part must be at least ten to twelve inches long or it will simply slip between the rollers. Even with parts that are of proper length it is not uncommon for the parts to move slightly when they are cut loose from the sheet. There are some programming techniques that can help should this occur. Parts should be oriented with their longest dimension perpendicular to the rollers. The cut on each part should be started in the center of the part where there is a roller on each side of the cut. Then, when the part is cut free, there is a roller holding each end of the part, which is more stable.

Another technique raises the cutter 10 to 20 thousandths about an inch before the part is cut free from the main sheet. This leaves a thin bridge between the part and the main sheet. This bridge prevents the part from moving during the final cut. In many cases, the machine can then reverse direction, lower and cut off this bridge. Since the bridge is very thin, little cutting force is developed and the chances of the part moving are reduced considerably. Parts too small to be properly held by the roller can be left attached to the main sheet by several of these bridges and then broken out by hand after the sheet is removed from the machine.

Very small parts can be machined using either vacuum or roller hold-down by not machining all the way through the part. By leaving a .010 to .015 inch web on the back of the part, the small parts can be machined easily. Then the sheet of parts is turned over and run through a wide belt sander to remove the web and separate the parts.

Early roller hold-down systems simply attached the rollers to the frame of the machine. The table bearings or the gantry bearings, depending on the machine design, resisted the clamping force of the rollers. As you increased clamping pressure to help the rollers hold the parts, you also increase the load on the axis bearings. This resulted in premature bearing failure in some machines. To address this issue, one manufacturer has installed a set of wheels that ride under each edge of the tabletop and pinch the table and parts between the rolls on top and the wheels underneath. In this arrangement the rolls add no load to the axis bearings regardless of the clamping force used.

Roller hold-down is commonly used when parts are to be cut from large sheets of material. In many cases, thinner material can be stacked and the entire stack cut at one time. Cutting irregular shaped parts from a full sheet of material can offer substantial yield improvements over cutting the sheet up on a panel system and then cutting the parts from the resulting blanks. When cut from a full sheet, parts can be nested to use the absolute maximum amount of material possible within the part itself.

There are several software packages that can assist in nesting a variety of parts based on production volume requirements. These nesting packages may either be able to run in the control, if the control is open architecture, or may be run on a separate computer and downloaded to the control. Each nest may be different and thus some type of universal hold-down system is needed. Since many times the material being cut cannot be held properly by universal vacuum, roller hold-down becomes the only alternative.

From an overall cost standpoint, mechanical clamps are the least cost method. These are followed by conventional vacuum and then universal vacuum. Roller hold-down tends to be the most expensive system. In the final analysis, however, the material and the part design may dictate the hold-down system rather than the system cost.

And now we will address the final area of a CNC router, the CNC control. This is likely the most technical and most complex of all of the technologies involved with this type of machine. In addition, this area is changing rapidly, so technical features that are not even imagined today, may very well be common in a year or two.

The very first machine controls were not CNC but were NC. NC stands for Numerical Controlled or controlled by numbers. These controls were electronic machine controls that responded to numbers that were input. The original machines read these numbers from punched paper tape. Holes punched in the paper tape corresponded to numbers. These were read by the control and then executed.

The early NC machines had no logic or control functions in the control at all. All information and techniques for operating the machine were carried by the punched tape program. This included functions such as acceleration and deceleration. Early machines tried to operate at the programmed feed speed instantly with no provision for controlled acceleration and deceleration. To prevent damage to the machine from these instant velocity changes, the programmer was forced to program short line segments at increasing speeds until final feed speed was achieved and then program additional short segments at the end of the motion each at slower speeds until the machine was stopped. The total length of all line segments then comprised the length of movement of the axis. As you can see, programming was an involved process with much opportunity for error.

Once a computer was added to the NC control it became known as a CNC control. CNC stands for Computer Numerical Control indicating that the control is equipped with its own computer. Although some very expensive systems based on minicomputers were being experimented with in the metalworking industry, the very first CNC control based on the newly invented microprocessor was introduced by Thermwood in 1976 into the wood industry. This system used an Intel 8080 microprocessor and allowed the control to calculate the acceleration and deceleration, making programming much easier.

Today, most but not all CNC controls automatically handle acceleration and deceleration. Things as simple as this were a major programming hurdle in the early days of NC. There is no reason today to buy a control today that has this major shortcoming.

As computer technology advanced, CNC capability increased. Each control manufacturer, however, developed the technology along their own proprietary lines. By the time the PC started to develop and PC standards were established, the machine control people had already established a different approach. The approach established for CNC controls was primarily intended to obtain strong real-time performance.

Real-time in the computer world means that not only does a process need to occur but it needs to occur within a specified period of time to function correctly. A PC type computer product is only concerned with performing a task. It is not concerned with performing the task within a specific period of time so that it can control something like a moving machine. Once a machine is moving the control functions must occur fast enough to keep up with the movement of the machine. Whenever a computing process must coordinate with a physical process it is known as a real-time application.

CNC controls were designed primarily for real-time computing. Early PCs were too slow and their operating software too inefficient to allow their use in the real-time machine control applications. Machine control was left for specialized proprietary CNC controls.

As PCs became more popular, many low cost peripherals such as hard disk data storage became available. These devices also held advantages for CNC controls, however, since the controls were not built using the PC standards, the devices could not be simply added to the control. For the control manufacturer to use the devices on their own products, they needed to develop the most fundamental interface and driver technologies for each individual device. The cost of this effort was high and the relative volume of CNC controls compared to PCs was quite low. As a result, the cost to the customer for a device, a hard disk for example, was ten to twenty times as much as the same device for a PC. Customers had a hard time understanding this.

At the same time the number of different devices coming to market was increasing dramatically. It was all but impossible for control manufacturers to integrate but a tiny fraction of the available technology. CNC controls seemed to be falling behind the fast advance of the personal computer industry.

Eventually the processing speed of PCs became fast enough that even with the poor real-time response of their operating systems, they were able to provide basic CNC control. At this point the CNC performance was substantially less than the existing proprietary controls however, they were now able to easily integrate peripheral devices. The machine customer was now faced with a decision. Should I buy a proprietary control that is incompatible with most of today's PC products but provides good machine performance or should I buy a PC based control that is compatible with much of today's low cost PC technology but offers a lower level of machine control.

This is where things get a little more complicated.

The manufacturers of proprietary controls quickly realized the threat that the new PC based controls held so they developed an approach to try and achieve some of the compatibility of the PC based controls. Instead of basing their controls on a PC they instead added a separate PC to the system and then connected that PC to their control through a serial line. The way this works gets a little complex, however, it does offer some of the advantages of the PC based control to the proprietary controls. It also creates some bottlenecks that could affect machine performance.

To understand these bottlenecks we must understand the fundamentals of how a CNC control processes part programs. A typical control structure maintains the part program in main memory. This memory offers very fast data transfer to and from the central processing unit or CPU. To execute a line of NC code, the line or block of code is read from memory, interpreted by the CPU and then converted to control instructions that are sent to the axes drives. Processing this block of data takes a certain amount of time. The time required to process a block of NC code is called block processing time.

In the past, block processing time was of little concern to the wood industry. A typical program was comprised of a few hundred lines of code, each representing relatively lengthy motions. With the increased use of CAD/CAM systems and the use of CNC routers for surfacing and carving, this is no longer the case.

The way that a CAD/CAM system creates a curved machine motion is to create a series of very short straight lines all connected together. These lines may only be a few thousandths of an inch long and there may be thousands upon thousands of these segments in a single curve. Executing this program now begins to create several problems.

The first problem that occurs is that the size of the program becomes very large. The overall program size is determined by the amount of CAD/CAM generated curved motion and the length of the straight line segments. Obviously the more curved motion the larger the program. Also, the shorter the line segment the more segments required per inch of motion and the larger the program. Shorter line segments generally mean smoother motion but at the cost of larger programs. Increasing the length of the line segments can reduce program size, but the result may be a rougher program.

Large programs create problems for many CNC controls. The first problem occurs when the program will no longer fit into main memory. Some method must be found for either breaking the program up into two or more smaller programs that will fit into available memory or finding some system for downloading the program into machine memory a segment at a time while the machine is executing. The most common way of doing this is to attach a PC to the control through a serial link. The large program is stored on the PC and then fed a segment at a time to the main control memory once the existing code in memory has been executed.

Although this system works, it creates some performance problems. With very short line segments and high feed speeds, data is executed at a high rate. Many times, this rate is faster than the ability of the serial link to transfer replacement data into memory. It is possible to run out of data to execute and the machine must stop and wait for new program data to load before continuing execution. These pauses in motion can cause quality problems when working in wood. They also slow program execution since the performance of the control determines cycle time rather than the cutting process.

Another approach that works well is the approach that Thermwood has taken in its SuperControl. They store the program on a very large hard disk that is part of the main control and then operate from the hard disk as if it were main memory. By eliminating the data transfers common with the other approach, virtually any size program can be executed as if it were located in main memory. Large complex programs no longer slow the control and limit production rates.

Another technical feature that becomes important in these circumstances is the speed at which the control can process a block of NC code. This is simply a measure of how fast the control can retrieve and execute a single line of NC code. It is called block processing speed and it determines the maximum feed speed of the machine executing a specific program. If block processing speed is ten milliseconds this means that the control is capable of executing 100 lines of code per second. If each line represents a segment .010 of an inch long, the maximum feed speed is one inch per second or 60 inches a minute. This is a relatively slow feed especially for a complex part such as a wood carving.

In general you need to use the longest line segment that will yield an acceptable surface finish and the fastest control you can get. Before the advent of CAD/CAM generated programs for wood, block processing speed was not particularly important. In three dimensional metalworking, feed speeds were slow enough that the control processing limitation never really came into play. Only when we began to try and execute CAD type programs at high speed did the limitation begin to impact performance. This is another area where the demands of woodworking far exceed the requirements for metalworking.

Thermwood's SuperControl points the way to the future of CNC controls. The architecture is not a PC based control nor is it a proprietary control. Instead it is a hybrid, combining the advantages of both systems into a single package.

This system uses a PC front end just like the metalworking controls, however, the PC is connected to the main control not through a link but by existing on the same internal buss as the main control. This makes interchange of data almost instant and causes the PC front end and the proprietary CNC control to operate as a single unit.

This architecture offers the compatibility of a PC with the raw processing power of a high-end proprietary CNC control. The control is capable of handling massive programs hundreds of megabytes in size, and it is capable of executing these at extremely high block processing speeds. This system also offers two features that have long been the goal of the control industry, multi-tasking and open-architecture.

These two features open a new world to CNC control and offer the potential for revolutionizing the wood industry once the capabilities are fully understood.

Multi-tasking simply means that the control can execute more than one independent program at the same time. Open-architecture means that a program that was not written by the control manufacturer can be executed on the control. Although both of these seem simple enough, the impact thay have on both capability and productivity can be substantial.

We take open-architecture for granted since it is the basis for personal computers. Every PC is inherently designed to run a variety of programs. It is difficult to understand that a CNC control is not like that at all. CNC controls are dedicated machines intended to run only the software written by the control manufacturer and no other. The control computer tends to be specialized making it perform very well but only in a rigid carefully controlled environment. Creating a CNC control that can also run other software is very unique today.

Multi-tasking has become somewhat commonplace with the advent of Windows NT and Windows 95 on desktop computers. Thermwood selected OS-2 as the operating system for its SuperControl because it has a much more predictable and more robust multi-tasking operation than any other commercially available operating system today. CNC controls operate in a real time environment and the ability to properly allocate processor time is absolutely essential.

On the surface, multi-tasking allows you to call up and edit one program while the machine is executing another. Real multi-tasking, however, holds promise well beyond this limited view.

An electronic operator's manual could be called up and procedures reviewed by the operator while the machine is in operation. The control could be placed on a network and messages sent and received by the operator while the machine is in production. A small video camera could monitor the cutting process inside the dust hood and display the resulting image directly on the control screen while the control is in production. The control could be queried in the background and complete data about the performance and production status could be uploaded across a network without the machine operator needing to assist the process. A separate program could keep track of the actual movement of each part of the machine and alert the operator to the need for lubrication or other routine maintenance only when it was absolutely necessary. A tool management program could keep track of the actual cutting time on every tool bit and alert the operator when the tool life has been exceeded. A CAD/CAM or other code generating program could be run on the control creating the next program while the current program is executing.

All of these capabilities are not only possible with multi-tasking but are actually being used in production on the Thermwood SuperControl. Most control manufacturers are currently working on their own hybrid controls with multi-tasking and open-architecture. Within a few years these capabilities will be commonplace and even more new innovations will be added to the list.

Another advantage of the PC based control or a hybrid control with a PC front end is that the part programs can be assigned alpha numeric names and can be stored in a directory structure. Most proprietary controls limit part programs to numeric names, which are not particularly easy to identify. When both letters and numbers can be used to name a program, it is much easier to locate the program you want.

The directory structure allows programs to be grouped in specific directories by design, type of part or finished product. With the advent of mass program storage, it is possible that a factory can generate and store in the control, thousands of different programs. Locating and identifying the program you want can become difficult and time consuming if you do not have a system that makes this easy.

An open architecture control should allow the installation of a bar code reader directly on the control. A bar code containing the key strokes necessary to load the correct program can be printed on top of the work order. With this arrangement, all the operator must do to locate and load the correct program is to scan the bar code. This process takes a few seconds and virtually eliminates program loading errors.

Another capability that is showing up on newer controls is the ability to execute parametric programs. Parametric programs are part programs where all required dimensions are not part of the original program. For example, instead of writing a program for a kitchen cabinet door that specifies the width and height in the program, we write the program using the word "width" and "height" in place of the actual numbers. These words are called variables. All dimensions are defined using the variables. For example the center of the door can be called "width divided by 2". As you can see this will give you half the width on any size door.

Once the program is completed using variables, you can assign actual numbers to "width" and "height" and machine a specific size door. You can then assign another set of numbers to the variables and use the exact same program to machine a different size door.

Kitchen cabinet doors are a good example of the power of parametric programming. A typical kitchen is made up of dozens of different sized cabinets each requiring a different size door. Using normal programming techniques, each different size door will require a new program. A particular door style may require over a hundred different programs to handle all the different sizes required. With parametric programming, a single program can not only manufacture every door needed but also any size in between.

In the past, parametric programming was used in a stand alone parametric CAD program, quickly creating all the programs needed for a set of cabinets. The problem is that you must first create the final execution program and then load that program in the machine control to cut the door.

To address this problem, Thermwood in its SuperControl has created a programming language called the Advanced Function Language. The Advanced Function Language or AFL is actually a full function computer programming language that can be incorporated directly into the NC part program. Using this program, variables can be defined, values assigned and mathematical functions performed. Parametric programs can be written using AFL and executed right on the control.

The Advanced Function Language offers much broader power than simple parametric programming. For example, not only can it define a variable but it can open a window and request that the operator input the width of the door which it than assigns to the program to cut the part. For an even more automatic operation, AFL could use a sensor to detect the edge of the door. Move an axis until the sensor detects the edge, use the position of the axis to determine the width of the door and automatically assign the dimension to the variable. With this system working, all you need to run any size door is to load the blank and press the start button. The AFL program measures the size of the door, loads the proper variables and cuts the finished product.

Using the Advanced Function Language, every part of the machine can be queried and controlled. Basic machine functions can be added for specialized applications. Truly, if you can imagine a function you wish to perform, you can very likely add it to the control using the Advanced Function Language.

Another feature of AFL is the ability to create macros. Macros are actual machine programs that can be assigned unused "M" or "G" code names and then they can be called by other programs. The real power of macros is very subtle but they are very powerful.

To understand the value of machine and tooling macros you must first understand how differences in the actual physical construction of CNC machines is handled by programmers. No two machines are exactly the same, however a machine with a single head will require very little effort to run the same programs on different machines. When a second or third head is added, problems become greater. It is virtually impossible to manufacture two or more machines where the spacing between heads is exactly the same. When a program switches from using head one to using head two, it must shift the heads to allow for the distance between them. Normally this shift is a motion within the program.

This program with the shifts between heads programmed in will only work on one machine. A second machine will require slightly different shifts between heads so it will require slightly different programs. This means that a program must be generated for every part for every machine. Five different parts that can run on five different machines will require twenty-five separate programs. This is getting quite complex.

One way of simplifying the programming effort is by using a CAD/CAM system. The Computer Aided Design or CAD portion of the system creates the actual part geometry. The Computer Aided Manufacturing portion of the system determines the tool path and tools required to manufacture the part. A final program called a Post Processor inserts the shifts between tools for a particular machine. A Post Processor program must exist for every machine. It contains the shift distances for that particular machine.

Now, a program can be developed all the way through the CAM system and then simply run through a different Post Processor for each machine it will run on. This simplifies program development but still results in twenty-five different programs that must be tracked and controlled so that the program is not run on the wrong machine.

Should a machine crash or a head change result in slightly different shift distances for a machine, the Post Processor must be modified to reflect the new distances and then all old programs must be re-posted using the new post processor. This can be a time consuming task when a company has thousands of existing programs. Again, accurately tracking the status of a program is difficult. An error will result in parts that look okay but are slightly off dimensionally.

Tooling macros address this problem in a different way. Instead of imbedding the shift distances in the actual part program, the macro is actually a short program that performs the shift. These programs are left in the machine but are called by the part program. For example you may have a tooling macro that shifts to tool two. This macro will have a specific name. The macro that shifts to tool two will have the same name on every machine even though the actual macro itself is not the same. Each macro will perform the steps necessary to shift to tool two on that specific machine.

The part program simply calls the appropriate macro to shift to tool two. It will perform the proper steps regardless of which machine the program is run on. Thus, the exact same program will work on every machine even though the machines may be physically different. An extreme example of this is two machines, one with the second tool mounted to the right of the main head and another with the second tool mounted to the left of the main head. Without tooling macros a totally different program will be needed for each machine. With tooling macros, the macro called by the program will shift the head to the left on machine one and to the right on machine two. The same program will work on both machines even though they are quite different.

In the case where a tool is remounted in a different location, it is only necessary to make a single modification to the tooling macro in the control for all programs to operate properly. It is no longer necessary to re-post all existing programs.

Another major benefit of tooling macros is that only one program exists for each part. That program will result in an accurate part regardless of which machine it is run on. The possibility of running a program on the wrong machine is totally eliminated.

This is a highly simplified version of how macros actually work in modern controls. The macro not only considers the tool it is going to but also the tool that is currently being used. The shift direction and distance will be different moving from tool one to tool two than if moving from tool four to tool two. Macros are also used to control spoilboard thickness, fixture location and a variety of input-output functions.

A control capable of handling macros can substantially simplify both programming and operation and will make errors much less frequent.

Thermwood's Advanced Function Language can go one step farther than a macro. Any set of program instructions can be given an unused "M" or "G" code name and essentially turned into a custom macro for a specific application.

Advancing control technology will be a key component to furniture manufacturing in the future. The production techniques that are evolving will rely heavily on advanced features of new age CNC controls. As computer technology continues to advance at an ever increasing speed, we can look forward to even more capable controls and even more possibilities for improved production systems.

Chapter 9

Processes

Chapter 9

Processes

A CNC router does routing, right? Well, yes… but today that is only part of the story. When a CNC router is used as the core of a Furniture Fabrication Cell, it must be able to perform every wood machining operation normally found in a furniture factory.

A modern CNC router can actually perform virtually every machining operation in a furniture plant provided it is properly equipped and programmed. In this chapter we will look at each of the typical processes and show how those processes can be performed on a CNC router. The processes shown here are not intended to be all-inclusive. As the Furniture Fabrication Cell evolves, new and perhaps better techniques will be developed. The processes shown in this book are intended to show the basics that have already been successfully used.

The first thing to recognize is that it will require either multiple tools or multiple heads or both to perform a variety of processes. In describing the various processes, we may show more than one way to accomplish a particular task. The actual selection of the process will depend on the machine configuration and final requirement.

Routing

The first process is routing. This is actually a very versatile process. As you will see, many other processes can be accomplished by slight modifications of the routing process. Routing is accomplished with a cutter bit rotating at high speed. The technology surrounding cutters used for routing has become quite advanced. These advances have led to tooling that offers faster feed speeds, smoother cleaner cuts and longer life.

Using the routing process, smaller parts can be cut from larger blanks. The resulting part can be either rectangular or have a freeform shape. If a straight flute cutter is used the edge will be straight. If a profile cutter is used, the edge will become profiled, however, at this point the depth of the cutter becomes important. The position of the tool above the tabletop when the cut is made determines the shape of the edge. Some edge profiles can tolerate variations while variations on other shapes may be quite noticeable.

If a fairly tolerant edge profile is being cut, variations in bit placement and part thickness may be accommodated. If the profile is not as tolerant, however, provisions must be made to accurately adjust the process.

Tool placement, that is the distance that the tool is placed in the tool holder, can be quite critical in many routing applications. This edge profiling process is one of those critical applications. The most obvious way of achieving an accurate depth is to load the tool using a depth gage. If you are quite careful you can load a tool within 0.005 to 0.010 inch. This will generally work for most applications.

If you require more accurate depth control, a tool measurement system can be put on the machine. Although not absolutely necessary for a Furniture Fabrication Machine, this feature is highly recommended because it virtually eliminates one source of possible inaccuracy and removes the possibility of human error from one area.

The tool measurement system generally uses a touch pad located just off the table. The head is stopped and moves over the touch pad. The head then lowers until the pad is contacted. At that point, the actual length of the tool is automatically entered into a tool table and the programs are all automatically adjusted for the measured depth of the tool.

The actual process of measuring the tool is somewhat involved. The most accurate system uses a touch pad that is actually a metal plate that has a small electrical voltage. When the router bit touches the plate, it electrically grounds the pad indicating contact. The actual measurement process grounds and releases the pad several times to determine the exact contact point. All of this occurs in a fraction of a second once the pad has been contacted so it is not noticeable.

The reason that the process of electrically grounding a touch pad is used is that it does not rely on any mechanical movement of a switch to define a position. Any type of mechanical or proximity switch has a band within which switch closure occurs. Sometimes this band can be quite wide. The electrical contact point using a touch pad is extremely accurate. This accuracy allows measurement down to a thousandth of an inch.

There is one major limitation to the tool measurement system. Because the system relies on electrical contact, the tool being measured must conduct electricity. Ceramic or diamond tipped tooling will not work with the tool measurement system. When these tools must be used, their depth must be accurately set off line.

The second area that can affect the edge profile is the thickness of the part being machined. If the part is too thick or too thin, the profile will be mismatched. The obvious solution is to plane the part thickness accurately. There is another approach, however, that will allow for any variation within a reasonable tolerance band. It will also take a reasonably accurate part and profile it very accurately.

The real problem with part thickness is that the tool depth is in reference to the tabletop. When the part is laid on the tabletop, the tool then references the backside of the part. The profile, however, almost always must be set to the front of the part. Thus, any variation in part thickness will cause a mismatch of the profile to the face of the part.

The only real solution, other than trying to maintain exact thickness, is to measure the front of the part and then adjust the program to the actual front face. This is done using a measurement system mounted to the router head. This system has several uses in Furniture Fabrication. Determining the exact location of the face of the part being machined is one of those applications.

The measurement process occurs just before machining begins and takes only a few seconds. This system is used for any routing process where the route cut depth must be referenced to the face, rather then the back of the part.

Another routing process, vein lining, is faced with a similar problem. In vein lining, a thin shallow cut is made in the face of the part, generally to accent a tabletop or similar product. The problem here is actually a bit more complex because not only must we adjust the depth of the cut but we must also keep the depth a set distance below the face of the part even though the face may not be completely flat. In this case, measuring the thickness of the part may not be adequate since any warpage will cause the position of the face to vary from one area of the part to another.

To address this application, a floating head is required. The floating head uses a foot that rides on the face of the part and determines the depth of the cut. It is a little like laying a hand router on the face of the part and then using the machine to push the router along the required path.

Shaping

The line between routing and shaping is not all that precise. As the diameter of the router bit increases, eventually the rotation speed must be reduced to keep the tip speed from becoming excessive and dangerous. These larger diameter slower speed heads at some point become shaper heads rather than router heads. At one point, the type of head determined if it was routing or shaping. A single piece tool with integral cutting edges was a router bit and a large diameter tool with interchangeable shaper knives was a shaper. Today, however, there are a number of different tools that blur the distinction between the two.

For our purposes, we will call any tool that operates in a router spindle as routing and any tool that operates on a shaper head as shaping.

The larger diameter of the shaping tool generally offers somewhat smoother edges and generally involves heavier cuts. Many times an even better edge can be obtained by shaping the edge and then taking a clean-up cut between 0.005 and 0.010 inch deep as the final cut. This effort may substantially reduce or even eliminate sanding although a routed or shaped edge normally will require sanding before finishing.

Heavy cuts will tend to put more force on the part so a solid part hold-down is very important. Any movement of the part will result in a poor quality cut finish.

Molding

Molding is shaping in a straight line with a special molding knife. Generally molding is the process of putting a shape on a long narrow part. This can be done on a CNC router in several ways. The most straightforward is to simply use a router bit or shaper with the appropriate profile and simply make an in-line cut along the part. Although this is not molding in the true sense, the final result is the same. This works well when the molding shape is small enough to be cut in a single pass. When the molding shape becomes larger, the final shape may require two or more tools that each cut a portion of the shape. On molding with a very large profile, there is still another alternative.

The molding is laid flat on the table top and a ball nose cutter is used to move back and forth along the length of the molding. Each time a pass is made, the cutter steps over and does what amounts to an in-line carving of the molding shape. Although this process is not as fast as making a single pass, it is actually a practical approach, especially when the final part is not extremely long.

This process has another advantage. With only a couple of standard tools, almost any molding shape can be cut without the need to have special profile cutters made. In small volume production, this can result in a substantial tool savings at the cost of a slightly longer cycle time.

By using the router carving capability, carved moldings can be produced in almost any design. The basic shape can be cut and then the detail carvings added using the techniques described in the carving section of this chapter.

Boring

Drilling holes in a part is a fundamental part of woodworking. There are two different methods of boring holes. The router itself can be used to bore a hole with a router bit provided the router bit has a plunge tip. Some router bits are designed to plunge directly into the work and others are not. If a non-plunge tip router bit is used to bore holes, it will generate excessive axial loads and may damage or destroy the router spindle.

Sometimes a smaller bit can be used to bore a larger diameter hole by creating a small diameter circle. Care should be taken when doing this to make sure the circular interpolation software used by the control will generate smooth accurate small diameter circles. All CNC controls do not generate accurate enough circles to perform this operation so make certain yours will before using this technique.

The second way of boring is to use a dedicated drill. It is common to mount a boring machine type 32mm boring head on a CNC router. These heads have a series of drill spindles on 32mm centers. The most common use of the 32mm drill bank is to drill several holes at the same time. In the zero-set-up world, however, there is a much more effective way to tool the drill bank.

The better drill banks offer the ability to raise and lower each drill spindle under program control. In this case, it is generally more efficient to equip each drill spindle with a different size drill bit. For example, a nine-spindle drill bank could be equipped with drills from 1/16 inch to 7/16 inch in 1/16 inch increments. The final two spindles could be tooled with a countersink and a counterbore bit. Thus, any size hole from 1/16 inch to 7/16 inch could be drilled without the need to change bits. A ½ inch or larger hole could be drilled using a router spindle and a ½ inch plunge type router bit.

Holes need to be drilled one at a time using this arrangement, however, holes are generally drilled rather quickly. The extra time required to bore the holes one at a time for an entire batch is generally much less than the time required to re-tool the drill bank between batches.

Mortising

A pure square hole mortise is not common on a CNC router. Several router manufacturers have offered mortise heads on their machines but these have seldom been used. Instead, an "H" mortise is routed into the piece providing a square opening to accept the tennon. The tennoned piece overlaps the mortise hole enough to cover the areas where the hole was enlarged by the routing process. This system is fast and effective and has been more popular in the market than adding a true square hole mortise head to the machine.

Edge Work

It is common to perform machining tasks on the edge of a panel. Panels can be edge bored, tennoned or dovetailed. The most common way of performing these tasks is to install right angle drills or router heads. The parts are fixtured flat above the tabletop and the necessary operation performed using horizontal tooling.

Although this system works, there are several disadvantages. First, Horizontal tooling is both expensive and somewhat maintenance prone. Fixturing the parts high enough above the tabletop to provide clearance for the horizontal heads can be both tricky and difficult.

One possible approach to the fixturing problem is a horizontal drill developed and patented by Thermwood. The fundamental problem with a horizontal drill is that the thickness of the bushing or bearing needed to support the horizontal spindle spaces the spindle shaft too far above the table. What is needed is a bushing with no thickness. To address this problem, Thermwood engineers simply made the drill housing out of bushing material so the shaft could operate properly without a bushing. The result is a drill that can bore a horizontal hole in the center of a ¾ inch thick panel lying flat on the tabletop.

Although this approach does eliminate the need for special fixturing, it still requires a separate horizontal head. For larger parts such as a dining room table, this is the only method that works well but for smaller parts there is another rather simple answer. The answer is a vertical table mounted to the side of the standard horizontal table.

Dovetail being cut on a vertical table

The vertical table is equipped with a conventional vacuum system or mechanical clamps. It holds the part so that the edge is pointed upward. In this orientation, normal vertical tools can be used to machine the edge. With this set-up, almost any edge work is simple and straightforward.

Sawing

A saw offers a fast clean way to cut off a part. The saw cut tends to be a little faster and removes less material than a router bit. The saw is restricted to straight line cuts and normally these cuts are along an axis.

A saw normally requires a separate slower speed head although systems are available where the saw is mounted to a tapered tool holder. A boss on the tool holder prevents the saw from rotating. To operate in this manner requires that the speed of the router spindle that drives the saw be slowed substantially. This slower speed results in a rather low horsepower head that might not be able to handle heavier cuts.

Saws tend to be used for groovibg on CNC routers more than for actual through cutting. In a Furniture Fabrication Cell, a saw can be used for mitering corners of moldings. It will generally perform this function better with less tear-out than a long router bit, which is the most common alternative.

Planing

A small planer head has been offered by at least one manufacturer and others are working on similar systems. With the popularity of curved and serpentine drawer fronts, the only really practical way of producing them is using a planer head.

This is a relatively new area of CNC machining and the full capability and potential of the process has not been fully explored yet.

Squaring

Squaring is the process of taking a routed inside corner that has the radius of the router bit and squaring the corner. The tool and process is patented by Thermwood and operates on a CNC router.

Squaring Tool

It consists of four scraper blades that oscillate back and forth from the corner. When these vibrating blades contact the wood they scrape the material from the corner toward the center of the part. The Squaring tool is machine driven through the desired profile and it removes the corner material leaving a square corner. In actual practice, the tool is first driven through a profile that leaves about 0.010 inch of material. It then make a second cleanup cut removing the remaining material and leaving a square corner that matches the router profile.

Carving

Router carving is another relatively new technology having been first introduced in the early nineties. For a CNC router to perform carving it must be able to handle very large files, must have fast block processing speeds and must operate with little or no lag error. The carving process consists of three or four different router bits. The first tool is generally a ball-nose cutter. It moves back and forth over the carving shifting .020 to .060 inch each pass. This tool defines the general surface of the carving.

A straight, flat bottom tool is used to square the bottoms of the carvings and a pointed detail tool adds the lines and detail. A smaller ball-nose tool and a smaller diameter flat bottom tool may assist in developing the carving on certain products.

The biggest technical problem with router carving is creating the large carving program. Early systems required the operator to move the machine through the carving sequence and the control recorded the operator's motions. Later systems substituted a separate programming machine that automatically performed the first ball-nose scan. The operator then added the squaring and detail motions to achieve the final product.

Current router carvers can both record the carving program and run production. An electronic probe is fitted with a stylist that is the same size and shape as the router bit. The machine then drives this probe over a sample part and records the smoothing program. The probe is then fitted with a square bottom stylist and moved by hand to create the squaring program. The probe operates the drive motors of the machine so there is little or no force required to move the machine around. The detail program is created in the same manner.

The manually created programs execute much faster than they are programmed so the programmer can slowly and carefully develop the program motions knowing that the machine will execute the motions as fast as possible regardless of how fast they were programmed.

The ability to carve is critical for Furniture Fabrication work. Not only does it produce detail carvings for fancy furniture, but the same techniques are used to create surfaces such as the drawer front of a Bombay chest or a wide molding. The lead-through-teach capability is also important if you are trying to accurately reproduce hand made furniture. A hand made part can be traced with the probe and all of the subtle inconsistencies will be accurately reproduced.

Unlike many of the other machining capabilities, carving does not require a special head. It does however require both a powerful CNC control and an extremely tight servo system.

Sanding

Profile edge sanding can be performed on a CNC router but the process is much more involved than most people believe. Few applications where parts are edge sanded have been successfully used because few companies understand the underlying technology.

Most sanding attempts have used a sanding wheel of some type that was pushed against the part and moved around the edge. The result was either burning of the part, clogging of the sanding wheel or very short sanding wheel life. In the end, most attempts have been abandoned.

At least two companies have developed sanding technology that does work on CNC routers if properly applied. These systems are already available from some CNC router manufacturers.

The single biggest fact that must be understood and accepted is that between three and five thousandths of an inch of material is all that can be removed in a single sanding pass. Any attempt to remove more than this amount will result in burning, clogging the sanding wheel and short sanding media life.

Once this fact is accepted, everything becomes much more complex. In order to control the amount of material removal to this tight a tolerance, every part of the shaping and sanding process must be controlled to a tolerance that is not normal in the industry.

The profile on the shaper blade must match the profile of the sanding strips within a thousandth of an inch or so. This tolerance is well beyond the capability of the normal equipment used to grind shaper blades within the industry. Currently, blades with the necessary tolerance are available from Voorwood as well as the matching sanding strips also manufactured within the same tolerance.

Even a process as simple as mounting the blades in the shaper body must be approached differently. For this process to work, the shaper blades must be positioned within less than a thousandth of an inch. A specially ground set-up fixture must be used to properly position the blades. Also, with the tight tolerances, shaper blades cannot be resharpened.

The CNC router that performs the shaping and sanding operations must be able to repeat the path dynamically within a very tight tolerance. Many machines are capable of very accurate static repeatability but cannot achieve the necessary level of dynamic accuracy needed to perform production edge sanding.

Production edge sanding is being successfully performed with good sanding media life. This only occurs, however, when the process is approached with a full appreciation of the demanding tolerances.

Dovetailing

Dovetail construction, which was common with hand made furniture in the past, is not commonly used today because cutting accurate dovetails has been difficult using conventional equipment. Machining dovetails with a Furniture Fabrication Machine, however, is as easy as any other type of edge work.

The easiest way to cut a dovetail is to use the vertical table, stand the part on edge and cut either a conventional dovetail or a long French dovetail using a dovetail router bit. The matching dovetail opening can be cut into a panel lying flat on the tabletop.

For dovetails to fit properly, the tolerance to which they are manufactured is rather tight. This is an area where the measurement sensor can be very important.

For example, consider cutting a dovetail slot into the face of a panel. This panel is fixtured on the machine tabletop. The router spindle can very accurately reference the tabletop, however, the dovetail must be accurately cut with respect to the face of the panel. If the panel is exactly the proper thickness, the dovetail will be machined correctly. If, however, the panel thickness is slightly off, the depth of the dovetail will be off by that same amount. Even small variations in the depth of a dovetail cut can cause problems.

In this case, the proper approach is to have the machine measure and verify the exact front face of the panel, adjust the program for that exact position and cut a perfect dovetail slot. The dovetail depth will be correct even if the thickness of the panel varies.

With the ability to measure and then cut very accurate dovetails, this construction method again becomes very practical.

Since the actual dovetails are determined by the program and not by a dovetail fixture, it is possible to achieve some effects that are not practical using more conventional means. The width of each dovetail cut can be varied to simulate hand cut dovetails just as easy as making all dovetails the exact same size.

In this section we have quickly covered several of the major processes already used in Furniture Fabrication. As this concept begins to be implemented, new demands will drive new developments. New processes and more efficient methods will certainly be offered. Even today, however, every process needed to build most wood furniture can be accommodated by a properly equipped Furniture Fabrication Machine.

Index

Index

A

B

C

D

CNC routing
  power required, 190
  conventional vacuum, 96, 194

E

F